THE ART
of the
BOOK
PROPOSAL

also by

ERIC MAISEL

FICTION

The Black Narc

The Kingston Papers

Dismay

The Blackbirds of Mulhouse

The Fretful Dancer

NONFICTION

Writers and Artists on Love

Writers and Artists on Devotion

Everyday Calm

Everyday Creative

Everyday Smart

Write Mind

The Van Gogh Blues

20 Communication Tips at Work

Sleep Thinking

The Creativity Book

Deep Writing

Staying Sane in the Arts

Artists Speak

A Life in the Arts

Fearless Creating

Affirmations for Artists

Fearless Presenting

Living the Writer's Life

20 Communication Tips for Families

JEREMY P. TARCHER • PENGUIN

a member of
PENGUIN GROUP (USA) INC. • NEW YORK

THE ART

of the

BOOK

PROPOSAL

ERIC MAISEL, PH.D.

FROM
FOCUSED
IDEA TO
FINISHED
PROPOSAL

Most Tarcher/Penguin books are available at special quantity discounts for bulk purchases for sales promotions, premiums, fund-raising, and educational needs. Special books or book excerpts also can be created to fit specific needs. For details, write Penguin Group (USA) Inc. Special Markets, 375 Hudson Street, New York, NY 10014.

JEREMY P. TARCHER/PENGUIN
a member of
Penguin Group (USA) Inc.
375 Hudson Street
New York, NY 10014
www.penguin.com

Library of Congress Cataloging-in-Publication Data

Maisel, Eric, date.
    The art of the book proposal : from focused idea to finished proposal / Eric Maisel.
    p.   cm.
    ISBN 1-58542-334-3
    1. Book proposals.   2. Authorship—Marketing.   I. Title.
    PN161.M26   2004   2003066342
    070.5'2—dc22

                    0 70, 52

Printed in the United States of America
10   9   8   7   6   5   4   3   2   1

BOOK DESIGN BY DEBORAH KERNER/DANCING BEARS DESIGN

Contents

THE ART

of the

BOOK

PROPOSAL

THINK BEFORE YOU WRITE

Millions of people want to write a nonfiction book. (Millions of people also want to write a novel. However, the strategies in this book are geared to the needs of the nonfiction writer.) If you are reading this book, you are probably a would-be nonfiction writer. You may want to write a memoir or a book that draws on your experience as a business consultant that you can sell to supplement your income. You may have a cookbook you want to write, or a self-help book arising out of your experiences as a chronic pain sufferer, or a local history guide about your small town in Colorado. What is most likely is that you harbor the desire to write a nonfiction book but that you haven't really gotten started yet.

Most of the people who dream of writing a nonfiction book and believe that they have something to say find it incredibly difficult to make a real start on their book. In their day job they may turn out manuals or other kinds of writing by the reams; they may have an advanced degree in creative writing; they may have kept journals for decades. But when it comes to getting their nonfiction book started, they can't. They can't find the wherewithal to make notes, play with titles, write some actual text, or begin in any way. Other people may leap in and write two hundred pages, only to look up one day to see with chagrin that their book isn't "working." They haven't crafted the book that was in their heart to create. Both the nonstarter and the leaper find themselves in deep trouble.

These first-time writers are not alone. Something very similar happens all the time, even to writers who have completed book-length projects before. Jane, who has written two nonfiction books, can't make any headway on her third, and for two years she wonders why she isn't writing. After doing a good job on three books, Bob makes a complete mess of the fourth. Mary decides to tackle something very large and finds that her previous ways of working are not sufficient. Barry attempts a sequel to his bestseller and the result is both false and deadly dull. These writers, even though successful in the past, do not start on their latest project. Or they work fitfully. Or they make a big mess at some stage of the process.

Why? What is going on?

Many things. The list of obstacles to writing a good book is longer than your arm. On that list you would find, for example, the stressors in your life, which prevent you from concentrating on your ideas. You would find the way you talk to yourself, which for most of us tends to be on the negative and self-defeating side. You would find your other daily life responsibilities, which steal time and mind space. And so on.

But very high on the list of obstacles is a blocker that you probably haven't recognized. It is the single most important reason why you may not have gotten very far on the book you'd like to write or are having trouble with the book you are currently writing. This block is the nature of the journey itself, the kind of task that writing a book is really like.

The short answer to the question "Why am I making so little progress on my book?" is that the journey from idea to completed book is among the most arduous on earth. It is hard work because thinking is hard work, and writing is about thinking, not physically making marks on a page. It may startle you to learn that a chess grandmaster expends as many calories during the course of a hard-fought tournament chess game as does a runner in a marathon. Thinking is literally that kind of hard work. It is hard work like digging ditches, only it is harder, because when you dig a ditch you know what you are doing. When you think hard in the realm of creating, you must make your choices in mental darkness, which is a terrific added strain.

THINKING AS STRAIN AND TERROR

Thinking is consistently experienced as a crisis state. We are alarmed to be thinking, frightened to be alone in a metaphorical darkness, terrified that our brain might be a quart short on oil and not operating properly. We predict that we will make a mess of our thoughts and think garbage. We worry that we will dream up dung instead of a beautiful book. As the author Kenneth Atchity explained in *A Writer's Time*, "Most of us hate to think. Five minutes of thought can be more terrifying, more energy-draining than days and days of routine activity." Although there are many obstacles to writing a good book, this is the primary one.

I've always been reasonably intelligent. But I only began to apply my intelligence to my writing relatively recently. I still only do so sporadically. This is natural and normal but a gigantic problem. To this day I send nonfiction book proposals out prematurely, before they are strong. Why? Impatience. Laziness. Wishful thinking. Greediness. The list is very long. The shorter list? Human nature. When I think about some of the proposals I've submitted to agents and editors, I cringe. What was I thinking? Well, I wasn't. I was hoping. I was hoping that an editor would give me a free pass and say, "There's potential here. We love you and we trust you and we'll buy your book on a wing and a prayer." That is truly what I had in mind as I sent wretched things out by post and got back form letter rejections two or three months later.

Working as a creativity coach and therapist to writers for almost 20 years, I have seen my clients and students do similar things. Teaching "getting your nonfiction book started" classes and writing classes for adults in a college setting, I have found that people often do not make a connection between writing and thinking. They would laugh if they heard someone advising a chess grandmaster to "just make any move, that'll get you started." Yet that is the message they seem to take away from books on writing, writing classes, and their own understanding of the writing process. "Write anything; anything is a start." I think writers pick up this message because consciously or unconsciously they wish that the writing process were easier than it turns out to be. They are stuck in wishful thinking.

We are all in this boat of not wanting to think. When my students, who are adults trying to earn their college undergraduate degrees after being away from school for many years, learn that they will have to write five long, smart essays in five weeks, they are almost all tempted to drop out of the program. I have to give them my "trust the process" speech and my "I will get you through this" speech—neither of which they believe right away. In fact, they are certain they won't be able to complete the course work. But then they do, because they are brave, because they are motivated, and because I show them how to think and write.

The joyous news is that once you crack through your own veneer of fear and come to recognize that you must think about your book if it is to come out right, you will enjoy the process of thinking. You will feel excited and motivated about your work. Well, to be completely honest, on some days you will feel proud and motivated. On other days, perhaps the majority, you may feel like whining and complaining, "I don't like all this thinking work!"

Once you accept that writing a good nonfiction book is hard work in the realm of thinking, that you are going to have to expend calories and devote brain cells to the process, and that you will have to face all of your fears about whether you can lavish real attention and discipline on an intellectual problem (for that is what a nonfiction book is), you will become a player in the creative game. You will have stepped up to the plate.

THINKING BEFORE WRITING

I'm advocating that you think about your nonfiction book before you begin to write it. I don't mean that you are to think about it in the sense of "Oh, wouldn't it be nice to write a book?" I mean that you will sit down and really think about your idea, that you will move it from its current vague state to the state where it is rich and fleshed-out. You will think about what you are trying to communicate, what form your book should take, what chapters it should be divided into, what should go into each chapter, what experiences you mean to draw on to substantiate it, what research you need to do to buttress what you know already, and so on. In the following pages, I will provide you with many exercises to help you do this and as much advice as I can muster. But the work will be all yours as you sit there, uncomfortable and anxious, demanding of yourself that you think.

The first days and weeks of the process may make you feel very uncomfortable as, instead of writing your nonfiction book, you force yourself to think about your book. You may feel unequal to the task of thinking so hard, you may start to call yourself names, you may dream up a million reasons why you are not entitled to write this book or why you should write some other book. You may question your expertise, you may doubt that the marketplace wants a book of this sort, you may announce that you don't really have anything to say. You may do every dance imaginable to stop the painful process of thinking. But at the same time, if you recognize that this is the process and that you are doing the right thing, if you can keep up your courage and your motivation, then one day some weeks or months into the process you will find yourself working on a good book. That payoff is guaranteed, if you can stay with the process.

You may be thinking, "I've read interviews with hundreds of well-known writers, and to a man and a woman they say that they do not think about their books, they just take dictation. They just sit there and their book comes out. So what is this guy saying? He doesn't understand at all." My response is that writers who are in the habit of thinking about their books do not notice that they are thinking about their books, in part because much of that thinking goes on when they are sleeping or resting or doing other things. They attack the problems their book presents them with, they think hard and long about those problems (sometimes for years), and then when they finally solve those problems they arrive at the experience that is often presented as "taking dictation." But they don't report the thinking part, maybe because it sounds unseemly to have sweated, maybe because they have forgotten or never consciously realized that they were doing it, or maybe because they just feel like pulling your leg about the writing process.

There is another reason why some writers fail to report the thinking part. It is that they don't want to examine their own process that closely. If they did, they would recognize some hard truths about the books they attempted that didn't work. They would have to confront the fact that some of the books that they began, often the ones closest to their hearts, did not receive enough of their best thinking attention and consequently sputtered and failed. I have enough of these books in my own life to know exactly what I am talking about. I can think of two recent books that went all the way to a completed draft stage, and several more that peeked into the world as book proposals, that I refused to think hard enough about and that consequently weren't good enough.

All writers fail in this way, and we don't want to tell anyone about it. So we smile and talk about the books that seemed to come from gods and muses. But if omitting the whole truth is lying, we are lying when we don't discuss how much thinking is required to write a good book and how often we don't want to do all that hard thinking. We are lying when we fail to recall how the first draft of a given book came out all wrong, and the second draft too, and that if we hadn't forced ourselves to think about what went wrong and what was still needed, we would have had nowhere to go but to the shredder.

Maybe we raced through the first draft not thinking much and just writing. But then, God bless us, we had to read that first draft. Then we got a tumbler of ice water in the face. The thinking work we had avoided earlier could be avoided no longer—unless, a sadder but not much wiser writer, we simply tossed the draft away and started on something new. Ultimately, there is no avoiding the work that must be done. That is thinking and bringing new meaning into the world.

CRAFTING MEANING

Just about every smart, sensitive person harbors the desire to write a book, because writing is a natural way for a contemporary person to use her talents, integrate her thoughts, express herself, and feel really alive. Maybe cave painting was the most natural outlet ten thousand years ago. Maybe story-telling around a fire served those purposes a thousand years ago. But for the past few hundred years the book has been the primary way for a person to get her meaning all in one place and hand it over to another person. So it's no wonder that almost everyone harbors the dream of writing.

It's easy to make fun of this desire when we look at a person who wants to write but doesn't write—terribly easy to call him or her a blocked, failed, impotent, foolish wannabe writer. But an inability to put together a strong book, even though one is smart, hard-working, and literate, is really a manifestation of an ongoing crisis. It is a special kind of existential crisis: an inability to effectively carve meaning out of the universe. The central task of the nonfiction writer is really the profound existential task of sorting through many meanings, selecting some particular meaning, and then advocating for that choice.

A book is a bit of newly minted meaning. It has a meaning focus: "Reader, you are to center your diet on grapefruit, you are to prepare yourself for the end of the world, you are to learn something about the banality of evil. By the end of my book, reader, I will have made some coherent meaning and I will have ignited a meaning fire in you." But if you as the writer haven't yet minted meaning, if you haven't gotten that far, you may find yourself saying things like the following to describe the book on your mind:

"I've led a really interesting life. I grew up in Poland before the War and, after I came to America, I made a lot of money. I should tell my story."

"I'm a very spiritual person but I don't find the books that I read about spirituality all that good. I should write my own."

"I teach molecular biology. That should be good for a book."

"I've been reading about the Civil War since I was eight. I should write my own Civil War book."

"I consult. Can't I write a book about consulting?"

Writing is about making meaning, and the following chapters will show you how to digest your material in such a way that your product has meaning for your reader. I don't want your thoughts and feelings undigested. I have plenty of those of my own. I need you to think, write, think some more, evaluate what you've written, discard what isn't working, write some more, think some more, have personal epiphanies of the sort that mean that you are suddenly realizing what your book is *really* about, and only then say, "Hey, bud, I've got something for you!"

Of course you can just sit down and write. Of course it's possible to write unconsciously and obliviously and get where you intend to go. If, working this way, you reach that psychological place we call a "block," of course you can simply wait for the block to dissolve and tell yourself that you are incubating your material, that you had better not force things, that you will write when you are inspired to write. No doubt wonderful books have come into being this way. But millions of books that might have been written are not written because authors and would-be authors pick this model, the laissez-faire model. If asked, they would say that they are "committed to process" or "honoring the process." But I wonder if it isn't fairer to say that, like me more times than I want to count, they have simply abdicated their job of wrestling meaning into existence.

You will have to decide this for yourself. If you are not writing the book you had hoped to write, if you are embarked on a book but it isn't really coming together, if you've tried your hand at a few projects but they never got completed or didn't match your expectations, I would ask you to think about changing your game plan. This book sets out a game plan based on the idea that writing a book of nonfiction is a difficult, dynamic enterprise requiring attention, planning, and thought. It requires your creativity as well, but creativity is not a synonym for "waiting for a visit from the muse." Creativity is an edgy, active, committed, passionate, full-bodied activity that requires your devotion and your willingness to be a meaning-maker.

I am still learning how to arrive at strong ideas, craft compelling book proposals, and make meaning. I have lots more to learn. But I have managed to write a few good books, I've sold twenty or more, and, as a creativity coach and teacher, I've worked with countless writers on their books and book proposals. I've also heard from writers who used the exercises in my previous books to help them conceive, write, and sell their nonfiction books. From these experiences, I have collected important guidelines to share with you about how to craft the sort of book and book proposal that will gladden your heart and make an editor's eyes open wide with interest.

A movement is needed from the place of no-meaning-yet to a place of meaning. Of course, you can get there just by writing. But I don't recommend it because I've seen too many people take many years looking for their meaning without finding it, whereas they could have made it or found it in two minutes flat if they had gone about it by asking themselves, "How can I marry what I want to say with what readers and editors want?" Just like that, they might have come up with the thread, the focused idea, the headline that allowed them to work in a passionate way on a wanted book.

DEFENSIVENESS AND SURRENDER

I recently received an e-mail from a freelance editor in Seattle who had been helping a client in California with a book that the client had been working on for *twenty years.* The client had six hundred pages done but no book in sight, and her editor confessed to me that, like all the editors before her whom this writer had hired, she couldn't seem to help this writer make any progress. But of course she couldn't. How could she? The writer in question was clearly unwilling to wrestle with her material. Until she found that willingness, until she surrendered to the work ahead of her, no outside agency could be of help to her.

A while ago I gave a role-playing workshop for a group of writers about how to communicate with agents and editors. During the course of one role play, a participant had the task of telling the "literary agent" across from him what his nonfiction book was about. But as hard as the agent prodded and probed, the writer just couldn't. Or wouldn't.

"So your book is about . . . ?" the literary agent would try.

"My experiences . . . personal essays . . . you know."

"No, not really. What kind of experiences?"

"Just some things . . . the old neighborhood . . . there were many interesting characters there . . . the things we did!"

"So, you mean, like a memoir? Is that—?"

"Well, not a book, more like a collection of essays—"

"Yes, I get that, but about what—?"

"Little pieces about my experiences . . ."

"Fine, but what does that *mean*?"

"Essays, you know—"

"Great. Terrific. Can you tell me about one of these essays? So I can get a sense of what—"

"Each one is different—"

"I know!"

"My experiences—"

"I know!"

Finally the writer surrendered. "Maybe this would help. Essays about Brooklyn in the fifties."

"Thank you!"

It would have been easier to pull out his teeth with bare hands than to get this writer to say, "My book is about *this*." His role-playing partner got more and more frustrated, as did the writer, who also started getting angry. It was as if being forced to say (or know) what his book was about was an attack on his being.

Most of us would be tempted to respond in the same way: it makes us terribly anxious to get right down to figuring out what we mean to be writing. But if we acknowledge and embrace that anxiety, it will simmer down. No writer is immune to anxiety, each must face it, and it erupts more forcefully the more we have at stake. This is why we can do work-for-hire writing without blinking but we balk at creating more personal writing. Since we don't care much about the former, we don't get very anxious. But since we do care about the latter, we get very anxious.

If you are in a writing group, you may have noticed that your fellow members can be very astute about noticing what is wrong with your writing but completely blind about their own. It is, after all, a thousand times easier to see the flaws in another person's work than to make our own work good. It's the difference between taking a car that isn't running and fixing it and thinking a car into existence. The first requires a mechanic. The second requires a dreamer, a creator, a thinker, an anxiety manager.

As soon as we feel that the writing we are contemplating matters, our defensive system kicks in, and our fear that we can't think well enough raises its ugly head. We are wrestled to the ground by the fact that we are trying to matter. To be fanciful about it, when we do writing for hire we do not suppose that we are doing anything sacred. As soon as we approach our own serious work, work that feels sacred, we are awed by the task we have set ourself, and we flee in apprehension.

The first step in creating your book is surrendering to the reality of the process. Do not suppose that you are writing a book. Substitute a new thought: that you are thinking a book into existence. Do not imagine that you know what your book is about and that all you have to do is write it down. Substitute a new thought: you have to learn what your book is about by thinking and writing. Do not imagine that you can get your book done well without willing yourself to plan, think, revise, organize, sweat, deal with confusion, and deal with anxiety. Substitute a new thought: that you will do whatever it takes.

GETTING STARTED

My goal in this book is to help you get the nonfiction book that you'd like to write off to the best start possible. By the end of our work together I hope that you will have a deep understanding of what your nonfiction book is really about and an excellent book proposal prepared. To start, the first thing I would like you to do is purchase two small desktop files, of the sort that can hold about a dozen file folders each, and three dozen file folders.

In the first file you will start to accumulate the notes you make about your book idea, completed exercises from this book, chunks of your budding book, and so on. In the second file you will start to build your book proposal (I'll discuss this in the next chapter).

Label the individual file folders for the first file as follows:

1. My Book Idea (and Variations)
2. Tables of Contents
3. Organizational Frames
4. What I'm Providing Readers
5. Titles and Subtitles
6. Various Chunks
7. Notes on Napkins and Jotted Down While Driving
8. Other Notes
9. Other Ideas (for Future Consideration)
10. Things Gleaned from Here and There (Articles, Clippings, etc.)
11. Older Versions of This Idea
12. My Latest Understanding of My Book

Next, do the following exercise:

Exercise : JUST THINKING

Tie your hands behind your back, so that you cannot possibly write. (You can do this literally or you can do it in your mind's eye.) Now think about your nonfiction book idea, the one that has been on your mind for some time and that has prompted you to purchase this book. (If you have no idea at all but simply have wanted to write a nonfiction book, just ask yourself, "Well, what might I want to write about?" When an idea comes to you that you think might be worth pursuing, choose that one to think about.)

Your idea may be extremely vague, like "a memoir," very concrete, like "a sequel to my last cookbook about cinnamon that focuses on nutmeg and that provides a nutmeg recipe for each of the world's 75 best-known holidays," or, most likely, somewhere in between. Whether your idea is vague or concrete, just think about it. You may be wondering "Think about it **how**?" You may be craving more instructions. There are more instructions to follow, whole chapters' worth, but no more instructions in this exercise. Just use your brain to think about your idea, dealing as you sit there with the natural anxiety that wells up when a person tries to think about anything.

Spend what will seem like an eternity thinking about your idea: say, ten minutes. Then untie your hands and write down your thoughts. Put these notes in the first file folder. When and if you feel like it, do some more thinking and some more note-taking.

If you got your file set up and if you completed the first exercise, you've made an excellent start. Congratulations! Please note that this book contains many exercises. While reading an exercise can often prove enlightening, this is less true with the exercises in this book. It is one thing to imagine creating two dozen titles for your book and another thing trying to actually create them. There is a big difference between agreeing that it would be a good idea to express your credentials well and sweating over their expression. Give the exercises a try!

Now it's time to look at the nonfiction book proposal. Let's take a closer look at what a book proposal is and why you will want to be working on it right from the beginning of the process of creating your nonfiction book.

THE NONFICTION BOOK PROPOSAL

The two files you've just set up—your "idea" file and your "proposal" file—are as intimately connected as conjoined twins. If, after thinking about your idea for a while, you discover that it has changed, so will your book proposal. Conversely, as you think about the demands of the book proposal, you are likely to discover that you want to make changes in the focus of your book that better reflect your expertise or that make it a more desirable commodity in the marketplace. Thinking about your book idea causes ripples in your book proposal, and thinking about your book proposal causes ripples in your idea.

THE NONFICTION BOOK PROPOSAL

You probably know that where prospective publication is concerned, a nonfiction book is usually shopped around before it is completely written. Nonfiction writers prepare a nonfiction book proposal, which describes their book to literary agents and editors. If an editor likes the book, she typically "buys" it—meaning, she makes an offer to publish it—without asking to see the completed manuscript; that is, she buys the book on the basis of the proposal. She purchases the book, then the book is written.

I have no idea who invented the nonfiction book proposal or who gave it its present shape. But somehow, the idea of a standard book proposal or a model book proposal began to infiltrate the writing and publishing consciousness. At some point instructional books about writing nonfiction book proposals began to appear. Perhaps the two best-known of these, the literary agent Michael Larsen's *How to Write a Book Proposal* and the literary agent Jeff Herman's *Write the Perfect Book Proposal,* appeared in the early 1990s. Today, most book proposals look reasonably alike.

While a nonfiction book proposal could theoretically be crafted in any number of ways, in the following pages I will present what has come to be considered the standard model because I think it is what editors are looking for. For example, editors have come to expect a hefty section describing what the author can contribute to the marketing of the book, so I will include a discussion of how to create such a section. If your goal is not just to write your book but also to have it purchased by a publisher, then while you could present your book in some other way and still sell it, you might be running the risk of having editors not bother with your proposal if it is missing some key elements that they are expecting to find.

The following are short descriptions of the 14 elements of a standard nonfiction book proposal. In subsequent chapters I will explore these elements in depth.

1. A *cover letter* (which accompanies the proposal) or a query letter (which precedes the proposal). This is the first thing an agent or an editor will see but the last thing you produce. The cover or query letter is clear and concise, it engages your reader's attention, and it convinces her that she should take the necessary time to seriously consider you and your book idea. This brief letter bears a lot of responsibility: it must lay on the table your major sales points (not only are you a master tart-baker but your tart cookbook comes with endorsements from Julia Child and Jacques Pépin) and meet any inchoate objections already forming in your reader's mind ("You may be thinking, not another tart book! But in fact only two tart books have come out in the last five years, and neither contained both savory and sweet tart recipes.").

2. A *clear organizing idea* with an unshakable center. This isn't a literal section of your book proposal but rather something that is communicated again and again throughout your book and your book proposal: in the title, in the subtitle, in the headline sentences you create to talk about your book. This idea is what your book is about and why it exists. If what you are writing is a book about the comforts of chocolate, then the idea of chocolate as comfort food is *everywhere* in your book and your book proposal. If it is a book about the dangers of chocolate, then the idea of chocolate as a dangerous food is *everywhere* in your book and your book proposal.

3. A *compelling title.* Many books, even many bestsellers, have unmemorable titles. But a book title that is also a resonant metaphor (like *Women Who Love Too Much, Jesus CEO, Midnight in the Garden of Good and Evil*) does the double duty of exciting readers and keeping the writer focused on her theme as she writes. Your editor and others at her publishing house may ultimately suggest (or demand) a different title, especially if yours isn't resonant, but it is still the writer's job to come up with as compelling a title as she can muster as early in the process as she is able.

4. *A useful subtitle.* Most nonfiction books come with both a title and a subtitle. The subtitle of *Jesus CEO* is *Using Ancient Wisdom for Visionary Leadership.* The subtitle of *Guerrilla Marketing* is *Secrets for Making Big Profits from Your Small Business.* The subtitle of Paul Theroux's book *The Great Railway Bazaar* is *By Train Through Asia.* While subtitles run the gamut—some long, some short, varying from very detailed to very understated—their goal is to provide additional useful information. If your title is obscure, indifferent, or weak, your subtitle can help a reader know what your book is about and encourage her to buy it. Even if your title is clear and strong, your subtitle allows you to add a second sales message and make a second pitch for your book. You can think of your subtitle as almost a dictionary definition of what your book is.

5. *A gripping overview of your book,* one to two pages in length, that communicates that your book is good, worthwhile, marketable, and really a book (and not merely a magazine article or newspaper story). In this overview you clearly state your book's central idea and you give a *brief* summary of why it is wanted by readers, who will buy it, how you will promote it, and why you are the right person to write it (items that you will discuss at length further on in the book proposal). Above all, you grab and hold your reader's attention.

6. *A format section* describing your book's organizational scheme. In this section you describe how your book will be structured, mention any additional features the book may have (illustrations, appendices, a forward by a well-known expert, etc.), describe its shape and size as you envision it, and remark on anything having to do with the book's general look, tone, and approach. At the same time, you communicate that you are savvy about the business by stating clearly that final decisions about the book's shape, size, feel, and particulars will be a publisher's. If you say that you must have 50 line drawings or a trim size that can fit in a purse, you are reducing your chances that an editor will read on if the production requirements you stipulate aren't compatible with her publishing house's vision or production capabilities.

7. *A section about the books that compete with and complement yours.* This section underlines your book's strengths, helps an editor categorize your book in her mind, and lets her imagine where in a bookstore your book will be shelved. It helps her locate it historically, as the latest in a succession of books. It helps her locate it intellectually, as a new wrinkle on an established idea, a new idea altogether, or an idea that connects other ideas. It places it in narrower contexts and in broader contexts: how your travel book about the Greek Isles relates to other travel books about the Greek Isles but also how it relates to travel books in general. Last, it demonstrates that special aspects of your book—illustrations, interviews, an unusually small or large format, and so on—should not be considered obstacles by pointing out that similar books have been successful in the marketplace.

8. *A marketing and promotions section* that assures an editor that book sales are in the picture and that you will energetically support your book. In this section you spell out the various markets for your book, both large and small, and especially those that an editor might not think of herself. You provide real market research and concrete numbers about your potential audience so that editors, who have neither the time nor the inclination to do the research themselves, are reassured that your book will sell. You also underline what you will do to sell and promote your book (as opposed to announcing what you hope the publisher will do) and paint a picture that leaves no doubt that you see yourself as an active partner in the selling of your book.

9. *A length and delivery date statement* in which you announce how long your book will be and when the manuscript will be ready. This section, which is often only a single sentence long, requires as much thought, planning, and cunning as much longer sections of the book proposal. There a monumental difference to you, in terms of the amount of work required and your time commitment, between a book that will be 60,000 words long and one that will be 90,000 words long, or one that will be completed in 10 months' time and one that will take two years to complete. There is also a world of difference to an editor, who may have an immediate need for a book like yours or a full roster of upcoming titles that would make it impossible to publish your book within the next two years, even if you had a finished manuscript ready in two months' time.

10. *A credentials section,* usually called "about the author," in which you tell an editor who you are and convince her that you are the right person to write this book and the right person to support it with marketing and publicity efforts. This section includes credentials you already have and those that you will acquire by the time your book appears. You may have led only a few workshops on the subject of your book, but you may have many more lined up: both items belong in your credentials section. You may have a mailing list of 20 or 30 people but fully intend to expand that list over the next year by joining online affinity groups, soliciting subscribers to your fledgling newsletter, and so on. The credentials section sets out the credentials you have and lets an editor know how you intend to beef them up in the future.

11. *A section in which you summarize each chapter,* also called an *annotated table of contents.* This section communicates that you know what your book is about, that you know what each chapter is about, that there aren't too few or too many chapters, that each chapter really has something to say, that your organizational scheme makes sense, and that your book flows from beginning to end. These chapter summaries can be very short, no more than a paragraph in length, or much fuller, as long as two pages each. They can also be prepared in a great variety of ways, as bulleted lists, using chapter excerpts, and so on. In chapter 10, I will look at 12 different methods of summarizing chapters that you haven't written yet.

12. *A sample chapter* that proves that you can write, organize, think, and do everything else required of an author.

13. *An endorsements section,* which is not always included but which publishers find increasingly useful. In this section you indicate which authors or experts you may be able to contact to obtain "blurbs," or endorsements, that the publisher can run on the back cover of your book. These days it's helpful to obtain a few endorsements ahead of time and include them with your proposal.

14. *A supporting materials section,* also not always included but useful. In this section you present a few carefully selected items that further show that your subject is of interest to people and that you are the right person to write and promote this book. You might present a workshop flier from a workshop you facilitated, an announcement of a talk you gave, clips of an interview you did with your local newspaper, or similarly relevant items. The purpose of these materials is not to overwhelm an editor with a litany of your accomplishments but to reinforce your central thesis: that people are interested in you and your subject.

The nonfiction book proposal typically runs anywhere from 20 to 80 pages, depending on how many sample chapters you provide, how detailed a job you do on your chapter summaries, and so on. If you are a celebrity, are an established author, have a very hot topic, or in some other way have a leg up on other writers, you may be able to prepare a bare-bones proposal that is just a few pages long and that does the trick. Indeed, if you are a celebrity you may only have to jot down your idea on a napkin. But generally speaking, editors need a full proposal in order to know whether they should go ahead and purchase your book.

COLLABORATING INTERNALLY

A book proposal is not just the essential sales tool of the nonfiction writer. It is also the essential teaching tool *for* the nonfiction writer.

Like wearing a back brace that causes you to sit up straight, the process of writing a proposal demands that you think about what your book is about and why another person would want to read it. By reminding yourself, at the start and throughout the proposal-writing process, that you are obliged to understand your book and its reason for being, you are less likely to drift away from the heart of your idea. If you put on your back brace and sit up straighter—that is, if you force yourself to preemptively answer the questions that literary agents and editors want and need answered—you will end up writing a smarter, more focused book that is more likely to be wanted by readers.

The demands of the nonfiction book proposal force you to understand the meaning in your book and articulate what your book is about, why you are the person to write it, and why anyone would be interested in it. These are exactly the demands that you should be placing on yourself from the very first moment of considering writing a book. The first month or two of creating your book should be all about investigating your idea *and* writing your book proposal. These are tasks that can and should go together right from the first instant.

It often happens, however, that a writer decides to do one or the other but not both. She decides, for instance, to think about her idea but to not think about the marketplace. If you go this route and, say, write in your proposal that your book will be about half a million words long and that an editor can help you trim it down to size, if any trimming is necessary, you will be able to hear the laughter all the way from New York. If you write that you are busy and that you can perhaps spare a little time to promote your book, editors will tell you not to strain yourself unnecessarily and that some other editor (perhaps on Mars) might be more interested in your proposal. If you turn a blind eye to the needs of publishers, they will turn a deaf ear to you.

A writer may, on the other hand, decide to focus and even fixate on the demands of the marketplace. She may attend every marketing workshop she can find, read *Publishers Weekly* religiously to keep tabs on trends, join writing organizations and study the marketing updates that arrive in her e-mail inbox, and so on. While this approach may help her produce a marketable product, the danger is that she will not think deeply about her material or her ideas and will opt, perhaps unwittingly, to try her hand at something trendy, formulaic, and opportunistic but not authentic. She may veer dangerously toward all sale and no substance.

Neither of these single-minded approaches is the best policy. But what happens most often is even worse: writers go to war inside and find themselves in deep conflict about whether they are writing "the book they want to write" or "a book that will be wanted in the marketplace." This simmering and sometimes raging debate saps motivational energy and causes writers to become blocked. On days when they suspect their book will not be wanted in the marketplace, they wonder why they are bothering to write. On days when they feel all the decisions they are making are marketplace driven, they feel they are betraying their art. On neither of these two types of days do they want to write.

You want a book that is rich and deep and you also want a book that you can sell. Your best plan is to make a pledge with yourself that you will keep your eye on both sides of the equation. When internal or external conflicts pop up—say, when you want to direct your book in *x* direction but you suspect that will make it harder to sell the book, or when an editor responds to a query letter by asserting that if you do *y* she will be willing to look at your book proposal—do not immediately take sides and let your stubborn "creative" head or your savvy "marketplace" head win the battle. Sit down with yourself, honestly consider both sides of the matter, and try not to bully one side or the other into capitulating.

One good way to do this is, at the beginning of the process, to devote yourself to your idea six days each week, then think about the nonfiction book proposal on the seventh day. On that day, read through the following checklist. Think seriously about each question and jot down notes to yourself in response.

Exercise : THE BOOK PROPOSAL CHECKLIST

Label a dozen file folders with the names of the 14 elements of the book proposal. You do not need one for "book idea," as the other file contains that information, and you should combine your notes on "titles" and "subtitles" together in one folder. Whenever you have a thought for one of these sections—say, a thought about how to express your credentials strongly or something that you might want to do to promote your book—jot it down and put it in the appropriate file folder.

It's a good idea to also make a folder called "book proposal checklist." Place inside it a photocopy of the following checklist and read the list once a week. You won't be able to answer yes to most of the questions on the list until you are near the end of the proposal-making process. But reflecting on them in a regular way will help keep your eye on current marketplace considerations without diluting the richness of your experience wrestling your idea into existence.

NONFICTION BOOK PROPOSAL CHECKLIST

By the time you are ready to show your book proposal to the publishing community, you will want to be able to answer yes to all of the following questions for each element of the book proposal.

ELEMENT 1. A clear organizing idea with an unshakable center.

- Has your idea stopped shifting around and settled into place?
- Do you have a single central idea that you can articulate clearly, simply, and directly?
- When you mention your idea to other people, do they exclaim "Nice!"?
- If your idea is still shifting and changing, has it at least settled down enough that you can clearly articulate it?

ELEMENT 2. A compelling title.

- Do you have a strong title for your book?
- Can you say in a sentence or two *why* it is a strong title?
- Does your title reflect what *this* book is about (and not what you originally intended the book to be about)?
- Does your title help interest a potential reader in your book?
- Have you tried out many alternative titles?

- If your book is the kind of book whose title ought to contain a "promise" or a "hook," does your title do that work?
- If your book is the kind of book whose title can be "literary" or "uninformative," is the title nevertheless strong and resonant?
- Do people seem to like your title?

ELEMENT 3. A useful subtitle.

- Have you spent as much time and attention developing your book's subtitle as its title?
- Have you considered many alternative subtitles in arriving at the one you like now?
- Does your subtitle add useful information and clarify what your book is about?
- Does your subtitle contain some "promise" or "hook" (especially if your title doesn't)?
- Does your subtitle reflect what *this* book is about (and not what some past incarnation of the book was about)?
- Do your title and subtitle work well together (i.e., if one is metaphoric or literary, is the other clear and informative, etc.)?
- Do people like your subtitle?

ELEMENT 4. A gripping overview of the book.

- Does your overview communicate that your book is *special, interesting, worthy, marketable,* and *meaningful*?
- Is it clear from the overview that your book is a cohesive book-length work and not a padded article or a collection of disparate fragments?
- Does every sentence, idea, and even word in the overview do some intentional work?

- Is the overview of the right length: namely, long enough to be convincing but not so long as to suggest that you can't be clear and succinct?

- Does your overview "steal" smartly from other parts of the proposal—that is, do you suggest how your credentials will prove useful, preview a smart marketing idea or two, compare your book in a useful way to a published book, etc.?

ELEMENT 5. A format section describing your book's organizational scheme.

- Is your book organized in a compelling way?
- Is your book organized in a logical way?
- Do you have a sense of how each chapter leads to the next?
- Can you articulate in your own mind the rationale for each chapter?
- Have you put in any unnecessary chapters or left out any necessary ones? If so, are you willing to double-check and make things right?
- Does your book include everything that a book of its sort ought to include (like strategies, exercises, and vignettes for a self-help book, maps for a travel book, a glossary for a book peppered with unfamiliar words, dramatic incidents for a memoir, etc.)?

ELEMENT 6. A section on competing and complementary books that provides a glimpse of the audience territory, underlines your book's strengths, and locates its place in a bookstore.

- Do you understand which books are "like" yours?
- Have you read—and at least glanced at—some recent books "like" yours that you can compare and contrast with your own?

- Have you shown how your book brings something new to the table that none of these other books bring?
- Have you shown the substantial, ongoing need for your book by highlighting how many successful books have appeared in your subject area (if that is the case)?
- Conversely, have you clearly explained how the need for what you're providing has so far gone unmet, if it has gone unmet?
- Have you helped an editor understand where in a bookstore your book will be shelved?

ELEMENT 7. A savvy marketing and promotion section.

- Have you carefully spelled out who you envision to be your potential audience?
- Have you provided real numbers, garnered from your research, about the size of your potential audience?
- Have you identified how these potential readers can be reached (e.g., periodicals they read with subscription numbers, support groups they belong to with membership statistics, websites they frequent with traffic information)?
- Have you identified the marketing and promotion efforts you intend to undertake?

ELEMENT 8. A length and delivery date statement, in which you announce how long your book will be and when it will be ready.

- Do you understand how long your book will be and *why* it will be that length?

- Do you have a good intuitive sense of how much time it will take you to write your book?
- Have you thought through answers to the following sorts of questions that an editor interested in your book might ask, and mentally calculated how such demands would alter your delivery date?
  - Can your book be shorter than you envision it?
  - Can your book cover more ground than it currently does?
  - Can you deliver your book sooner than the time specified in your proposal?
- Have you decided whether you will work on your book while it is being shopped around or whether you will turn your attention to another project?
- If you have decided to work on your book during the "shopping" period, have you created a writing plan and a schedule?

ELEMENT 9. A credentials section, in which you tell the editor who you are and convince her that you are the right person to write—and represent—this book.

- Have you made excellent use of rhetoric and language so as to present yourself in the most favorable light possible?
- Have you helped yourself look like the expert you will be at the time of completion of your book?
- Have you carefully mentioned any credentials that, while not directly related to this book, help make you look professional and interesting?

ELEMENT 10. Chapter summaries, in which you
communicate that you know what your book is about,
that it flows, and that each chapter really has something
to say.

- Have you gotten "inside" each chapter and learned conceptually what you intend it to do?
- Have you made use of the ways chapters can be summarized to create the best chapter summaries possible?
- Have you carefully walked the line between presenting too little information in each chapter and too much?
- Would a stranger be able to get a real sense of what each of your chapters contains by reading your summaries?
- Do the chapters "add up" to a compelling, intriguing whole?

ELEMENT 11. A sample chapter that demonstrates that you
can write, organize, think, and do everything else
required of an author.

- Is your sample chapter long enough? Is it too long? If your chapters are very short, do you need to include more than one in order to provide an adequate sample of your book?
- Is the sample chapter you've chosen the smartest one to include? Does it do an excellent job of selling your book?
- If it isn't the first chapter, did you include a sentence or two explaining where the chapter fits into the whole of the book?
- Is the sample chapter representative of the other chapters in terms of length, style, and content?
- Is the sample chapter wonderfully organized and written?

ELEMENT 12. An endorsements and testimonials section, in which you name potential endorsers and relay what endorsers have already said about your idea or the work you do.

- Have you brainstormed a list of potential endorsers of your book by looking at the work of other like-minded authors or prominent authorities in your field?
- Have you obtained one or two strategic endorsements already?
- For potential endorsers who are well known and/or not personally known to you, can you articulate how you would reach them?

ELEMENT 13. A supporting materials section, in which you present relevant materials, like clips, interviews you've given, workshop fliers, and so on.

- Have you included any carefully selected items that help make the case that you or your idea is already of interest to people?
- If you don't have such items, can you get them, by giving a talk, for example, or publishing an article?

ELEMENT 14. A cover letter or query letter.

- Is your cover letter or query letter brief and to the point?
- Is it convincing?
- Is the central idea of your book perfectly clear?
- Have you described your strengths as an author and salesperson?
- If a stranger proposed a book like this to you, would you be interested in looking at it on the basis of what this letter had to say?
- Is your letter a model of courtesy and professionalism?

HELP YOURSELF STAND OUT FROM THE CROWD

Writers fear that the odds against them are too long. There seem to be too many writers and too few publishing slots. But in fact, as Simon & Schuster editor Rebecca Saletan explained in *Book Editors Talk to Writers,* "one of the biggest misconceptions people have about editors is that we're surrounded by masterpieces, trying to decide which of them to publish. We don't. We sit surrounded by masses of not-so-good writing and stuff that's just okay. I'm looking for something that absolutely captivates me." This is great news for writers, because by doing the work outlined in this book you can make your book proposal stand out from the rest.

When I mentioned to one of the editors with whom I work that I teach classes in book proposal writing and that I was writing a book on the subject, she exclaimed: "God bless you!" Editors need better proposals from us. They need us to do several kinds of better work: better work in envisioning and understanding our book, better work as writers, better work as advocates for and exponents of our book, better work *across the board* as thinkers, writers, and promoters. If you do that better work, you will write a good book and greatly increase your odds of selling it.

YOUR BOOK IDEA

Whether you have been working on your book for months and have hundreds of pages written or whether you only have a vague idea for a nonfiction book, it is my experience that the exercises in this chapter and the next two will be of benefit to you. I'll offer a variety of ways to help you move from vagueness to a fully formed book idea or to further focus and hone your existing idea. There are several exercises in these chapters, and I hope you will attempt them all. I anticipate that it will take you a couple of weeks to do the exercises, learn from them, and maybe do some of them more than once.

If you are a writer who is just beginning, you may be daunted by the way your book idea keeps shifting in these first weeks and find it frustrating to proceed. If, on the other hand, you have a lot of your book written, you may grow sad as you work the exercises and perhaps discover that you have a better, deeper, or different way to proceed with your book. If you feel frustrated, sad, or otherwise down on yourself or the process, remind yourself that your goal is to write a good nonfiction book. Remember that you are trying to mint new meaning, really use your brain, challenge and test yourself, and live your largest dream.

WHAT IS A FOCUSED BOOK IDEA?

"Love" is a vague idea. "Young people today are more frightened of love than the young people of previous generations were" is a focused idea. The beginning of a focused book idea might sound like the following: "I could write a book called *Love and Terror,* in which I try to get at the extent to which fear is the central problem for young people today, maybe with chapter titles like 'fear of intimacy,' 'fear of loss of control,' 'fear of betrayal,' 'fear of boredom,' and so on."

"High divorce rate" is another vague idea. "It would be nice to know if today's high divorce rate is actually a positive thing and a function of new-found human freedom, with people free to leave marriages as soon as they no longer suit them," is a focused idea. The beginning of a focused book idea might sound like the following: "I could write a book called *The Freedom to Divorce* based on interviews I conduct with divorced people, interviews that focus on how they found getting out of their marriage to be a life-saving, liberating, and maybe even spiritual experience."

Can you see the logical progression from vague idea to focused idea to focused book idea?

What you will need, if you are to write and sell a nonfiction book, is a focused book idea and not just a vague idea or even a focused idea. To help you better understand what a focused book idea is, consider the following 20 examples. Each example contains three different but related embryonic ideas. Feel through what distinguishes one idea from the next. For each, try to answer the following three questions:

1. Does a way to frame this material instantly pop to mind?
2. What would make this idea hard to sell?
3. What is the central strength of this idea?

I'll offer some thoughts on the first one. You try your hand at the next nineteen.

TWENTY IDEA THREESOMES

1. a. A book about a person's experiences surviving a Nazi death camp. *Thoughts:*

(1) Probably chronological. But maybe it could be organized around vignettes of characters the narrator encountered in the camp. Or maybe it can start with the liberation and be done as an extended flashback. I can also sense how it could be organized around the seasons of the year or around a metaphor like "death and rebirth."

(2) "Yet another" survivor story. What makes this one special?

(3) Still an evergreen subject after all these years and full of built-in pathos and drama. One of the central events of the last century.

b. A book about a person's experiences in escaping from a Nazi death camp. *Thoughts:*

(1) Chronological, probably, maybe divided into three parts: getting to the camp, planning the escape, and the escape itself. Or it could focus very tightly on the escape, say just the day of the escape, minute by minute.

(2) So many "escape" books and movies have been done.

(3) A basically thrilling subject, made doubly memorable by the fact that so few people managed to escape from the camps.

c. A book about a person's experiences running a Nazi death camp. *Thoughts:*

(1) Something other than strict chronology would be good. Some organizing metaphor, perhaps around sin and redemption. Or the writer could focus relentlessly on the idea of horror, juxtaposing the nightmare lives of the prisoners and the nightmares of the camp commander in a book called something like *Nightmare.*

(2) Lack of empathy for, or downright hatred of, the narrator. The narrator is so far on the "wrong side" of the issue that it is hard to see how he can redeem himself.

(3) Fascinating, exciting, and even breathtaking to hear from such an archetypal villain. If the book turned out to be something other than a whitewash job, potential for enormous insights into human nature.

Now it's your turn:

2. A book about

(a) the two best retirement cities in America.

(b) the twelve best retirement cities in America.

(c) the three hundred best retirement cities in America.

3. A book about

(a) the first woman to win the grueling Trans-Alaska dog sled race.

(b) the second woman to win the grueling Trans-Alaska dog sled race.

(c) the third woman to win the grueling Trans-Alaska dog sled race.

4. A book about

   (a) investment strategies for women.

   (b) investment strategies for actors.

   (c) investment strategies for homeless people.

5. A book about

   (a) a woman who marries a toll collector.

   (b) a woman who marries the Prince of Wales.

   (c) a woman who marries a woman.

6. A collection of essays about saving the rivers of

   (a) North America.

   (b) Italy.

   (c) Argentina.

7. A book about

   (a) the problems of commuting.

   (b) the future of commuting.

   (c) how to grow spiritually while commuting.

8. A book about cooking with

   (a) ginger.

   (b) onions.

   (c) tangerines.

9. A book about

   (a) accountants' dreams.

   (b) writers' dreams.

   (c) celebrities' dreams.

10. A book about

   (a) anger.

   (b) why women are angry at men.

   (c) effectively releasing your anger using a five-step program.

11. A book that teaches children that

   (a) all religions are to be respected equally.

   (b) there is one true God and one true religion.

   (c) there is no God.

12. A book

   (a) of interviews with alien abductees.

   (b) that mocks alien abductees.

   (c) that coins a term—say, hysterical alien worship syndrome (HAWS)—for the peculiar madness displayed by putative alien abductees.

13. A book about

   (a) 65-year-old parents and their 40-year-old children.

   (b) 40-year-old parents and their 15-year-old children.

   (c) 15-year-old parents and their infant children.

14. A diet book

   (a) about eating sensibly and exercising.

   (b) advocating melons as the secret to weight loss.

   (c) that argues that overeating is the result of food allergies.

15. A guide to using

   (a) Netscape 5.0.

   (b) Netscape 6.0.

   (c) Netscape 7.0.

16. A book

   (a) examining Lincoln's Emancipation Proclamation.

   (b) analyzing Lincoln's depression.

   (c) collecting Lincoln's favorite venison recipes.

17. The experiences of

   (a) a woman who was raped by her brother when she was six, and her lifelong battle with depression.

   (b) a woman who was raped by her high school swim coach, and the trial that ensued.

(c) a woman in Bosnia who was raped by soldiers when she was 60 and who subsequently started Bosnia's only rape counseling clinic.

18. A book

(a) about psychic healing.

(b) debunking psychic healing.

(c) by a celebrity psychic healer.

19. A book

(a) identifying the cheap restaurants of Provence.

(b) about eating at cheap restaurants in Provence.

(c) about starting a bistro in Arles.

20. A book about walking as

(a) meditation.

(b) exercise.

(c) self-therapy.

Exercise : INVESTIGATING YOUR BOOK IDEA

If you already have an idea in mind, whether it's a vague idea, a focused idea, or a focused book idea, try to answer these same three questions:

1. Does a way to frame your material instantly pop to mind? Do some alternatives also come to mind?

2. What would make your idea hard to sell?

3. What is the central strength of your idea?

Answer these questions fully. Does one organizational scheme seem more logical or compelling than another? Does the central strength of your idea seem to outweigh its potential sales difficulties or do the sales difficulties feel like serious obstacles that outweigh the *inherent strength of your idea? Think about your answers—which may result in you provisionally elevating one version of your book idea to first place in your mind—and put your notes in your growing "current idea" file folder.*

SOME THINKING, SOME WRITING, SOME NOT KNOWING

When I begin on a book, it is with something like a vague idea, a feeling, a hint of what I want to write about. That's all I know, that's all I have to start with. Maybe, for example, I have the feeling that no one has set out to investigate the problems that creative people face in their intimate relationships. I say to myself, "That would make for an interesting book!" This is the vague idea stage.

What typically happens once that vague idea arrives and we have the sense that we might like to work on it is that questions begin to swirl in our brain. For me, considering the book on artists' intimate relationships that I just mentioned, which I'll dub *Artists in Love,* the following questions begin to simmer:

- Would an editor be interested in *Artists in Love,* or would she—correctly or incorrectly—feel that the market for such a book would be too small?
- Do I know enough about the subject? I've seen lots of creative people as a therapist and creativity coach but precious few couples. When it comes time to get down to brass tacks, will I have enough to say?
- Can I get a handle on this subject? Am I going to discover that a big relationship book of this sort takes me all over the map, that it has no center, nothing I can really grasp?

- Am I going to have to research a million famous couples and find something to say about each of them? Do I have to go back over the Lilian Hellman–Dashiell Hammett ground? Or can I skip that?

- Do I have to write two books or divide my book into two sections, one about creative people in intimate relationship with creative people and one about creative people in intimate relationship with noncreative people? Do I have to worry myself about that distinction or can I choose the former and just run with it? Or maybe the latter is really the one to focus on?

- Do I have to deal with all of a creative person's personal relationships—with her audience members, her literary agent, her mother, her son, and so on—and not just with her significant partner? What are the pluses and minuses of broadening the canvas and letting everyone in?

- Am I directing this book to the creative person? Because I could also write it for the noncreative mate: "Look, Harry, this is why Mary spends 48 hours straight in her studio and then sleeps for 14 hours." Who is my audience?

- Has something like this book been done?

- Will I be creating too many false distinctions between putative creative people and putative noncreative people? Are they really so different, one from the other, or are they really both just human beings? Where do I stand on this central question?

- What about bisexuality? Gay artist couples? Should I get into that? Would that be an added strength or a minefield (or both)?

And so on.

These are the right questions to be pondering. Unfortunately, we virtually never look at them directly. They swirl around, unsorted, all mixed together, each stepping on the toes of the other. Because of this chaos, we feel blocked. Or else we rush to write, almost to drown out these good questions. If I were to write these questions down and try to answer them, I would be doing my book-to-be a terrific service. I would be getting potential problems out of the dark of a noisy mind and into the light of a clean piece of paper. I might be able to answer each one in turn, or begin to answer it, or at least alert myself to the problems inherent to this book, problems that I should keep an eye on as I proceed.

Do I ever actually write out a list of this sort when I begin a book? No. Nor, I suspect, do you. I think we are frightened by our doubts and worries about the project we are incubating and, for defensive reasons, don't feel able to look at our own good questions and our own potential objections. When I say that you should think about your book from the beginning, I don't mean that you can think your book into existence. It must be written into existence. Rather, this is the sort of thinking I mean. Let's begin.

Exercise : YOUR OWN GOOD QUESTIONS

You can do the gentle or rough version of this exercise.

■

GENTLE QUESTIONING

Imagine that you are sitting by a river when suddenly a muse in a flowing dress—Musette is her name—floats down and comes to rest beside you. Enter into a pleasant conversation with her. She will ask you what your book is about and you will try to tell her. Every once in a while she will scrunch up her face and say, "I don't understand." Try to help her understand. If she has any doubts or objections, try to meet them. If she has any suggestions, think about them and see if they seem to have merit. You will want to be a scribe and record this dialogue as it is taking place, so that you don't miss any of her good questions or your good responses.

∎

ROUGH QUESTIONING

Imagine that your idea is a murder suspect. In your mind, be a tough cop and give it the third degree, as if you and it were in a gangster movie from the 1940s or an episode of **NYPD Blue**. Do not let it get away with any inconsistencies. Poke holes in its story. Make it confess to the kind of book it wants to be and what it means to contain. Occasionally change your tactics, become a good cop, and try to seduce further answers. When it breaks and admits what it intends to be, give it a yellow legal pad and say, "Are you ready to write that down?" Then write down what your book intends to be. If you can't get a complete confession, note any lingering problems or inconsistencies that remain.

When you have finished this exercise, think about what just transpired and try to put together a list of questions that reflect your doubts, concerns, or wonders about your budding book. Then put your list aside for some hours or overnight, as it may be too taxing and anxiety provoking to try to answer them right away. Remind yourself that you are just thinking about your book, not coming up with final answers, and that you have more exercises to do that will clarify matters.

When you feel ready, review your questions. If some answers come to you, write them down and congratulate yourself. If nothing but questions remain, do not worry.

WHY BOOK IDEAS CHANGE THEIR SHAPE

A would-be nonfiction writer may feel that the book idea she has in mind is self-evident, even though she hasn't investigated it yet. She may have a sure sense that she knows what she means by "a book about walking as meditation" or "a book about eating at cheap restaurants in Provence." But when she tries to start writing her book, she is likely to discover that she doesn't really know what her book is about.

Even if her idea is very focused—say, "a book about the 12 best retirement cities in America" or "a book that advocates melons as the secret to weight loss"—she is nevertheless unlikely to have much of a clue what her book will actually contain, how it should be organized, what tone she should adopt, and even whether she can stand behind her 12 choices of retirement cities or her melon advocacy once she begins to really think about and write her book.

Is her book on retirement communities a book intended for people in their fifties, sixties, or seventies? For all three? If so, do members of these age groups all have the same needs and wants? Does she have anything to say not said in books already on the shelves? What if the melon-book writer comes upon an article that argues that eating too much melon causes cancer? Will she ignore it? Must she include physical exercises in her melon book? How technical should she be about nutrition and body physiology? How can she stretch her single idea into a book-length work? It turns out that the realities of these two books are still ahead of their writers, even though each possesses a focused idea.

Consider the next wrinkle. The following are four embryonic ideas for a memoir:

- A narrative by a woman whose father was Thailand's best-known auctioneer and who followed in his footsteps to become Thailand's first female auctioneer
- A narrative by a woman who was stricken down by a mysterious illness a week before her wedding, causing her fiance to break off the engagement and sending her into a 10-year depression
- A narrative by a woman who discovered that her overeating was a spiritual problem and that by creating a fasting retreat she was able to lose a hundred pounds
- A narrative by an immigrant to America who arrived with $23 in her pocket and became a leading motivational speaker

What I hope occurred to you is that all of these books might be the story of *one and the same* woman. And I hope you're staggered by the implications of this possibility. If each of these descriptions represents a perfectly fine embryonic book idea, which one ought the writer to tackle? What is her memoir to be about *really*? You might say, "Well, if she's careful, she could make each idea into a chapter and take care of the problem of an abundance of ideas that way." But what if our would-be memoir-writer didn't become an auctioneer until the very end of the story, after her motivational speaking career ended? What if her spiritual awakening, which happened in her forties, had roots that occurred in her teens and had to be alluded to early in the book? What if, in short, the ideas could not be neatly separated, unwound, and talked about separately, as one might unwind the coils of a rope and display each coil separately, but had to be talked about all coiled together?

This, of course, is more like the way things really are. It might be desirable to extract one focused idea from among these several ideas and craft a narrative around that idea. Conceivably that could be done. But a reader would probably feel that something important was missing from the narrative. Ideas are not like eggs in a carton, each sitting up neatly in its own cavity, that can be extracted and sold separately. They are more like spices that individually disappear into a dish and come together to produce a subtle curry. Most books must contain many ideas, because of the way ideas interlock, so you must become easy with the notion that there is a long journey ahead of you as you work to combine your ideas in just the right way.

Because your first vague but pregnant idea (to write a memoir) is likely full of these other ideas (what it was like to be Thailand's first woman auctioneer, how you managed to find spiritual peace after decades of searching, how you discovered your own idiosyncratic weight loss program, what it was like to be abandoned by your fiance because you became ill, and so on), you will discover that your first attempts to get the right combination of spices together (there being no recipe and no clues whatsoever) are likely to frustrate you. The answer? To accept that this is the process, to be brave, and to will yourself to keep thinking about your book even as your anxiety mounts.

Virtually every nonfiction book has the nasty habit of shifting, changing, morphing, vanishing, reappearing in new dress, and not quite settling into place as the writer thinks about it and begins to work on it. She may start out believing that she is creating a book on Celtic mythology and end up writing a book about her adventures in Venezuela, as strange as that sounds. Her book on parenting may become a book on grieving. Her memoir may shift its focus away from the time she was raped and toward the early years of her unhappy childhood. Her self-help book, which she thought was about chronic illness, may turn out to be about the saving grace of a lifelong devotion to creativity. Writers are confronted by this shape-shifting all the time: it is the norm, not the exception.

Here is another example. A student in one of my book proposal writing classes, a minister about to retire, sent me the following e-mail between week 3 and week 4 of our eight-week class. "After much deliberation," he wrote, "I have changed the topic of my nonfiction book radically. I've envied those in the class who intend to write about their personal experience. Not only does this sound easier than my topic, *The Psalms and Celtic Spirituality,* but it sounds more interesting. So now I want to relate the highlight experiences of the 10 work brigades I led to Central America, in a book I'm thinking of calling *The Road to Guazapa.*"

In fact, it wasn't because his new idea seemed more personal or more interesting than his old idea that this writer changed his mind. Rather, he was groping for a place to make meaning, and this new place—stories about his experiences in Central America—seemed more promising than an academic study of Celtic mythology. You can bet that when he actually begins to tell his Central American stories, he will be confronted by another meaning crisis, because he still doesn't know *why* he is writing this book or *what,* on the level of meaning, it is really about.

Fledgling writers get extraordinarily frustrated as they find the center of their nonfiction book failing to hold. They do not know the true nature of the idea they are wrestling with or why they have chosen this particular topic to write about. They tend to react to this common problem—which they do not know is common and which they think is a failure on their part—in one of two ineffective ways. They feel blocked and stop writing, telling themselves that they have no right to write this book. Or they lurch along for years, manufacturing chunks of writing that do not fit together, because the chunks belong to different versions of one idea or to different ideas altogether.

Book ideas shift and change for all sorts of reasons. Consider the following example. A woman with a focused idea came in to see me. She owned a company that forecasted technological breakthroughs, and in that capacity she knew the top executives of America's largest companies. Concerned about environmental issues, she wanted to find out for herself to what extent major companies had instituted ecologically sound policies and whether those policies had affected the company's bottom line in a positive way.

Because of her access to top executives she was permitted to conduct interviews with the managers charged with responsibility for their company's environmental policies. Her idea was to write a book that summarized her findings and convinced top executives to make their companies "lean and green." She imagined that a small professional press that targeted executives would be the sort of press to search out, and she already had a few leads in that direction.

I agreed with her "lean and green" premise but not her book idea. I argued that the book should be for everyone, for consumers and employees as well as for corporate executives. Wouldn't consumers love to know which companies were greenest? Wouldn't it incite CEOs to make their companies greener if they knew that consumers would learn about their efforts (or lack thereof)? Wouldn't it be nice to provide employees at every level with strategies for improving environmental awareness at their company? At first she disagreed with me, then she wasn't sure, then she agreed, then she agreed enthusiastically. By the end of our 90 minutes together she had her book idea—one radically different from the one she had walked in with.

In the first example, the about-to-retire minister switched from one idea (about Celtic mythology) to another idea (about work brigades in Central America) because he had no focused idea yet and maybe no idea beyond wanting to write a book. In the second example, the writer had a focused idea but her book morphed as soon as she accepted that she needed to change her vision of her audience, from company executives to everyone.

Consider a third example.

Say that you start out with the following idea: "Berkeley in the 1960s was a hotbed—no, *the* hotbed—of radical activity. I'd like to look at that, because something about that time resonates for me. Maybe I could examine one aspect or another of the Free Speech movement, retell the story of People's Park, or focus on some obscure but important radical of that period. I'm sure I could make meaning any number of ways, using Berkeley of the 1960s as my locus and touchstone."

You begin to read about that place and that period. You start writing a book about Harry Moscowitz, an obscure radical. Quite by chance, you encounter the following fact: that Berkeley in the 1930s was the world seat of nuclear physics exploration. You recognize that a book could be written about that, too, focusing on the personalities of the physicists who came to Berkeley, the striking events in the history of physics that occurred during that period, the tensions between physicists and the military as World War II commenced, the petty rivalries among the physicists, and so on. However, none of that particularly interests you. But some vibration is set off by encountering this information, and you find that your book about Harry Moscowitz is no longer progressing.

A week later the following idea pops into your head. "Smart people are the most dangerous people in the world, because they have the ability and the curiosity to bring things like the atomic bomb into existence. Berkeley attracts those people. But smart people are also the world's salvation, because they have the highest principles. Berkeley attracts those people, too. *This* is interesting. What if I argue that Berkeley is the most dangerous place in the world and also the world's salvation? I could do a cultural biography of Berkeley like nothing that's been done before!" This is the creative process at its best and morphing as blessing.

ACCEPTING THAT YOUR BOOK WILL MORPH

Whether your ideas morph because they are moving in the right direction or because you yourself are at sea and drifting, the fact remains that your idea is likely to shift many times during the early stages of the thinking-and-writing process. Be ready for this and try not to let these stomach-churning shifts stall you or derail you.

Exercise : YOUR CURRENT IDEA AND ALTERNATIVE VERSIONS

One way for you to surrender to the fact that your idea may shift many times is to consciously articulate various versions of your idea. For example, for the **Artists in Love** book I mentioned at the beginning of this chapter, I might come up with the following five versions, each of which focuses on a different concern.

1. *Artists in Love: A Complete Relationship Guide for Creative and Performing Artists and Their Intimate Others*
2. *Artists in Love: What We Can Learn from Twelve Famous Artist Couples*

3. *Would You Marry an Artist? A Complete Guide for the Significant Others of Creative People*

4. *Artists in Love: The Seven Keys to Making Relationships in the Arts Work*

5. *Writers in Relationships: Everything You Need to Know to Deal with Your Editor, Your Writing Group, Your Literary Agent . . . and Your Significant Other*

Sit with the notes you have made so far about your book idea and think through five (or more) alternate versions of it. For each version, write a paragraph (or a least a few lines) about the central intention of a book with that focus, what material it might contain, and how it differs from the other versions. You do not need to select among these versions yet, so feel free to generate as many versions as you like. The one you ultimately settle on may be the first one you come up with or the eighth. Try to produce an abundant number of idea versions that match the many different ways your idea might be handled.

Now that you've spent time thinking about alternative versions of your book idea, let's look at several other ways of transforming your vague idea into a focused book idea. How will your book idea change if you decide to take the needs of your reader into consideration? How will it change if you want to write a book that is more secular or one that is more existential? How will shaping your material around an organizing metaphor affect your book's central idea? I examine these and related matters in chapter 3.

FINDING YOUR FOCUS
AND YOUR FRAME

After doing some thinking about your book idea, perhaps you can see much more clearly what your book intends to be. Maybe you can state its central focus and list some of the material you want to cover. But probably many questions still remain. Say, for example, that you intend to write about "the 12 best places to retire in the Southwest." Will you take your reader on the road from one potential retirement locale to the next and engage in a breezy narrative about the sights along the way? Or will you take a serious tone, as if you were a lecturer at a university? Will you organize your book by states, or according to the size of each community, or alphabetically, or in some other fashion?

What about facts and figures? Will you provide them or just make mention of contact information? Will you include anecdotes that you gather from retirees or will you leave out first-person reports? These and scores of similar questions will need answering before your book finally settles into place. Even though you have the clear idea that you will be writing about 12 specific cities and towns, what the book actually contains and the best way to organize it are probably anything but clear.

It's also possible that instead of having arrived at a clear idea for your book, you now realize that it might be any one of several different books. It might be "the 12 best places to retire in the Southwest," but it might also be "Sunbelt retirement on a shoestring" or "hidden retirement gems in New Mexico" or "desert living after 60." Which of these will you choose to write, and why? The topics covered in this chapter will help you consider ways of framing your book, should your idea be clear to you, and help you pick one of your ideas to focus on, if you have several competing ideas that interest you.

THINKING ABOUT YOUR READER

Unless you have a coerced reader, like a student in a class who must read your assigned text, anybody who picks up your book is also free to put it down. Metaphorically speaking, many people "put down" the book they have just read even though they managed to read it all the way through to the end. They forget it instantly and never return to it, because it made no impression on them. It failed to add anything rich to the meaning in their life. The book was well made enough and contained enough information or incident to keep them going, but as soon as they were done they mentally placed it in their "used books to sell" pile.

Think about this reader. Dream about her putting your book in a place where she intends to return to it again and again. Yours will be a reader favorite. Yours will be the cookbook she actually cooks with, the one she always pulls down when company is coming. Yours will be the memoir she recommends to her friends. Yours will be the travel book she gets off the shelf when the winter rains make her pine for Greece. Yours will be the self-help book whose program she actually works. Yours will be a book that matters in her life.

Thinking about this reader, ask yourself right now, "What do I hope she will get from my book?" One of my students, who was considering writing an actors' survival guide, answered this question in the following way.

TEN THINGS I HOPE TO PROVIDE TO READERS

1. Provide acting students and actors with the hard facts of what it's like to be a working actor.
2. Universal experiences common to actors. Rehearsals and daily activities such as acting exercises.
3. Lessons learned and how to avoid common pitfalls or mistakes in auditions and performances.
4. How to approach a role.
5. How to deal with a difficult director or situation.
6. How to learn to memorize.
7. How to get past fears (if actors ever do).
8. Learning to listen and trust.
9. What actors feel is the most important thing about their profession.
10. How actors work successfully with each other.

Producing this list did not immediately clarify in this writer's mind how his book would be organized or what it would be about. But it did force him to think hard about his book. The phrase *Provide acting students and actors with the hard facts of what it's like to be a working actor* made him wonder whether a "downer" theme of this magnitude should be his main order of business. The phrase *How to get past fears (if actors ever do)* caused him to consider whether he meant to write a self-help kind of book and, if he did, whether he was qualified and knowledgeable enough to do that. The phrase *How actors work successfully with each other* brought up the question of whether this might be more a relationship book.

As you can see, this writer ended up with more questions than answers. But they were good questions, questions that needed answering. A reader who might never return to his book as he originally conceived it, or even read it in the first place, might return again and again if it focused on providing useful information about actors' relationships, say, or if it described an arsenal of smart self-help tools.

Exercise : TEN THINGS YOU ARE PROVIDING TO READERS

What do your readers need from you? What do you want to offer them? List 10 things that you would like readers to get from your book. Sit with your list and think about how each item on the list affects your book idea. For example, you may discover that there are several clear principles that you want readers to understand, which might suggest that you organize your book around those principles. Or you may discover that you want your readers to focus on one main point, which places in question some of the other material you had wanted to include.

Expect that you will be raising questions rather than finding answers. Do not worry if it seems that no single book can provide every-

thing that you've listed. Maybe no single book can. But by the same to-
ken, maybe by the time you arrive at your final book idea you will have
found the way to provide most, if not all, of the items on your list.

SECULARIZING AND EXISTENTIALIZING
YOUR MATERIAL

Any book can be conceived as a "more practical" or a "more philosophical" book. Where your book falls along the spectrum of very secular to very existential is part of its basic design and basic intention.
You can fill your cookbook with existential overtones or you can make
your exploration of subatomic physics so chatty and nontechnical that
a lay reader will give it a chance. That's the writer's choice.

A definition of *secularize* is "to convert to lay use." For every reader
who is looking for a philosophical treatise on the meaning of money or
an exposé of brokerage house practices, there are a thousand who want
to know how to pick winning stocks. For every reader who wants to
read about arcane controversies in medieval theology, there are a million who only read books about contemporary spiritual practices. These
are reader realities—and therefore literary agent, editor, and writer
realities too. While you may want to write in a very existential way,
even if that is your inclination it is still a good idea to learn how to secularize.

Some writers secularize automatically. Their personality is such
that they naturally keep the needs of readers in mind. Other writers
learn the value of secularizing as they go along. Novelists who were
reporters first, like Hemingway, learn something important from their
newspaper experience about how to keep a reader along for the ride.
They learn to take out the adjectives and the semicolons and to meet a

reader's need for speed. Most writers, though, are not very aware of this secular-existential continuum and so may write at the existential end of the continuum simply because they haven't learned the skill of secularizing. If they choose to write at that end of the spectrum, that is certainly their prerogative. But if they are trapped there because they do not understand how to convert what they know to lay use, that is merely unfortunate.

You secularize by how you write and also by how you frame your material. The more complex the plot of your novel, the more you may lose your reader. The simpler the plot—the more it is *boy meets girl, boy loses girl, boy gets girl back,* or hero faces amazing obstacles but eventually saves the day—the more you have secularized your plot. Not only is most of Hollywood built on the idea of secularizing material but so are the greatest works of literature. We are more interested in murder than robbery: if Raskolnikov had merely stolen the moneylender's cash and not murdered her, we would be measurably less interested in *Crime and Punishment.* We are more interested in stories with a love interest than stories without one: if *War and Peace* did not revolve around the love triangle of Andrei, Pierre, and Natasha, would readers have flocked to that novel for its battle scenes alone?

Consider how you might go about secularizing a memoir.

1. You can contrive to make your life story into something practical by offering advice about some issue central to the memoir, like anger, anorexia, alienation, and so on. You might include the opinions of experts and describe what resources were available to help people with this problem. In short, you could move your memoir toward self-help nonfiction. The secular maneuver here is a *shift in genre.*

2. You could contrive to make your memoir "simpler" by focusing on one major period in your life, one crisis, one adventure, one theme, and so on. This narrowing is secular in the sense that a reduced version of anything is easier to comprehend, digest, and use than the messy, comprehensive version. The secular maneuver here is a *shift toward simplicity.*

3. You could maintain a tone of hopefulness throughout your memoir, end it on a positive note, and put an optimistic spin on your material. The more positive and hopeful your tone, the more secular your book. The secular maneuver here is a *shift toward lightness.* While dark books sell and even sell beautifully, the general rule is that human beings prefer fairy tales, happy endings, and feeling good.

4. You could use plot and incident in your memoir to produce resonances that remind us of well-known stories, resolving conflicts in ways that are familiar to us (even if they didn't end so neatly in real life), using elements of the mystery novel or the romance novel, and in a multitude of ways make it easy for us to read along. The secular maneuver here is a *shift toward convention.*

5. You could remove descriptions, pare down details, employ short sentences, leave out subplots and side issues, and in a general way get rid of any obstacles that interfere with the pace of our reading. The secular maneuver here is a *shift toward speed.*

6. You could employ an organizing metaphor that helps readers link up the parts of your story. Your device could be a theme like "women who love too much," a recurrent image, like Günter Grass's packets of fizz powder in *The Tin Drum,* a physical locale, like the river in *A River Runs Through It,* an ongoing distinction, as between the pace of things in Mexico and the pace of things in the United States in *On Mexican Time,* and so on. The secular maneuver here is the *use of organizing themes and metaphors.*

In constructing your nonfiction book, you will be making choices about utilizing or not utilizing a secular shift. Will you leave out certain incidents from your memoir because they seem too dark and you're angling for lightness? Will you add layers of "unnecessary" complexity because your narrative seems too simple and untruthful without it? As your book takes shape in your mind's eye, you can angle it toward the secular or away from the secular.

It is neither good nor bad to secularize your material. Rather, there are powerful reasons to opt for secularization and powerful reasons to avoid it. You may be inclined to avoid it for fear that you will lose nuance, depth, complexity, and truthfulness. You may be inclined to embrace it because secularizing your book increases your likelihood of interesting editors and readers. Your goal is to find a happy balance point, one where you can go deep but still give readers the accessibility they want.

Consider the following example. Sally, an avid ocean rower who takes her scull out into the harbor every day and who periodically rows in open ocean races, believes that she has something to say about the growing sport of ocean rowing. Among the first choices she must make, as she thinks about the book about ocean rowing that she might write, is whether it will be more about "how to row" (the secular approach) or more about "what it means to row" (the existential, metaphysical, spiritual, or intellectual approach). Thinking about this, she arrives at four possible versions of her book. They are, from most secular to least secular, as follows.

ROWING BOOK 1 (MOST SECULAR)

IDEA: Encourage women to adopt ocean rowing as a lifetime sport.

TITLE: *A Woman's Guide to Ocean Rowing*

SUBTITLE: *Everything You Need to Know to Make Ocean Rowing Your Lifetime Sport*

TABLE OF CONTENTS

1. Why You Should Row
2. The Basic Mechanics of Rowing
3. Ocean Rowing Versus River Rowing
4. Choosing Your Boat
5. Boat Safety
6. Learning About Weather
7. Learning About the Ocean
8. Moving from Harbor to Open Ocean
9. Competitive Ocean Rowing
10. The Big One: Crossing the Ocean
11. Rowing as Lifetime Sport
12. Rowing Resources

NOTES: very secular, with resources on rowing clubs and rowing equipment, a bibliography of recommended rowing books, and a breezy, straightforward style

MEANING THREAD: a vision of women turning to rowing

ROWING BOOK 2 (QUITE SECULAR)

IDEA: Communicate how rowing can become a spiritual practice.

TITLE: *Rowing Toward God*

SUBTITLE: *The Seven Principles of Sacred Rowing*

TABLE OF CONTENTS

Principle 1: God Is a Verb

Principle 2: Rowing as Meditation

Principle 3: Rowing as Spiritual Exercise

Principle 4: Rowing as Chi Activator

Principle 5: Rowing as Odyssey

Principle 6: Rowing as Riddle and Koan

Principle 7: Rowing with Heart

NOTES: even though about spirituality, a secular book, because its goal is to help readers connect rowing and spirituality in a practical way

MEANING THREAD: spiritualizing rowing in a practical way

ROWING BOOK 3 (SECULAR BY VIRTUE OF ITS ORGANIZING METAPHOR)

IDEA: Get at the allure of ocean rowing by organizing the book around the history of a particular race, the annual Long Beach–to–Catalina "holy grail" of ocean rowing regattas.

TITLE: *The Great Rowing Race*

SUBTITLE: *From Long Beach to Catalina with Speed and Grace*

TABLE OF CONTENTS

1. Marker 1
2. Marker 2
3. The Great Man Drops Out
4. Marker 3
5. Marker 4
6. The Other Woman
7. Marker 5
8. Marker 6
9. When the Finish Line Is Water

NOTES: rooted in reality, full of names, dates, places, and events, and organized around the race, so secular, but lyrical, meditative, and artful

MEANING THREAD: the race as metaphor at many levels

ROWING BOOK 4 (UNSECULARIZED)

IDEA: A collection of essays about ocean rowing, held together by the author's voice; the kind of book a columnist for *Existential Ocean Rowing Magazine* might write.

TITLE: *The Blue*

SUBTITLE: *Reflections on Skimming Over Water*

TABLE OF CONTENTS:

1. The Life of a Boat
2. From West to East
3. The Lost Pairs
4. Ecstasy
5. On Bringing Bach Along
6. Why Women Row
7. Docks and Boat Houses
8. Rowing to Alcatraz
9. The Last Rowboat

    (and 20 other brief essays)

NOTES: a book that reviewers might liken to jazz

MEANING THREAD: each essay a facet of the multifaceted diamond that is ocean rowing

Exercise: IMAGINING VERSIONS OF YOUR BOOK
ALONG THE SECULAR-EXISTENTIAL
CONTINUUM

Just as I did for the ocean rowing book, try your hand at imagining and describing a handful of books based on your idea—say, between four and six versions—that move from the most secular way you might treat your material to the most existential. For each version, use the format I used:

IDEA:

TITLE:

SUBTITLE:

TABLE OF CONTENTS:

NOTES:

MEANING THREAD:

When you have your four, five, or six versions completed, think about them. Try to articulate for yourself the pluses and minuses of each approach. Feel through which is closest to your heart to write and which would be most wanted in the marketplace. If they are one and the same book, you have your book idea. If they aren't, you will have choices to make and more thinking work to do.

As a reader, if I am looking for a book on investing, I know I want the *most* secular book on investing I can find, the one that provides the most information and the best information. If I want a basic book on gardening or home decorating, I want one that is secular: I want to know what grows in my climate or how to choose the right blinds for the den. In another mood I might read the works of Kierkegaard, or an impenetrable French postmodernist, or a tome on the physics of time, or some other very nonsecular book. I choose what I read according to my needs, my desires, my moods.

When I write, I try to strike a balance between the secular and the existential. My goal is to convert what I know to your use without oversimplifying. As a writer, you have choices to make along the same lines. You can turn the identical material into a text for a philosophy class or into a popular read. You can do quantum theory for your physicist peers, for undergraduates, or for the interested lay reader. You can organize your memoir around a single metaphor or you can give us your life story day by day and blow by blow. As you look in your mind's eye at your unwritten book, you will want to try to fathom where along this continuum you mean to be.

METAPHORIC RESONANCE AND ADDED DEPTH

How are nonfiction books organized? In the previous section I showed how one book about ocean rowing might be organized around basic how-to strategies, a second might be organized around seven principles of sacred rowing, a third might be organized around the events of a particular race, and a fourth might be organized as a collection of brief essays.

There are a great many excellent ways to organize a nonfiction book. You might organize your self-help book around steps or core principles. But you also might organize it as more of a narrative with, say, the story of your recovery from addiction taking center stage. You might organize your history of the Spanish Civil War around three sets of diaries, one from a Franco follower, one from a Spanish communist, and one from a New Yorker in the Lincoln Brigade. Or you might organize it very differently, say in a chronological way that follows the major battles of the war. You might organize your personal memoir into chapters named after popular songs and then employ musical metaphors throughout your narrative. Or you might organize your memoir as a series of vignettes spotlighting interesting people you have known. These strategies and countless others are available to you.

However, certain organizing schemes have more metaphoric resonance and depth than other organizing schemes. If we organized our book about gardening around holidays like Valentine's Day, the Fourth of July, and Thanksgiving, we might set up associations in a reader's mind, causing her to associate gardening with love of a spouse, love of country, and love of family. If we organized our book about resistance to Nazis in wartime Belgium around the fate of one trainload of prisoners escaping to freedom, we might be able to layer our narrative with resonances from other freedom rides, like those of the Underground Railway during the time of slavery. In these ways we might be able to add metaphoric resonance and depth to our nonfiction book.

How do we hit upon a felicitous metaphor or image? Primarily by reminding ourselves that we are looking for one. Consider the following example. Imagine that you want to write a book about the Spanish conquest of the Native Americans of New Mexico. You want to write this book for a variety of reasons, including the fact that your family was on the "wrong side" in the conquest and you would like to make a certain kind of amends by telling the truth about those times. You could tell a narrative history of the conquest and allude to your family. You could tell a narrative history of your family and allude to the conquest. You could weave one story with the other. You could fictionalize your family's story and write a novel. Any of these approaches might work.

As you think about these matters, you remind yourself that an elegant solution to your problem, one with depth and metaphoric resonance, is your ultimate goal. You remain open to the arrival of such a solution and hold off from choosing any of your current ideas, as they seem second best. You continue dreaming up possibilities and trying them on for size. Then one day the answer comes to you. You realize that you can construct your book as a history of the grand hacienda near Sante Fe where your family once lived. That hacienda will serve as the central image of your book.

You can show how that monument to good living was also a monument to conquest and oppression. Your book will be time based but not strictly chronological: you will start with life at the hacienda from 1900 to 1910, when it was expanded and remodeled, showing it as a happy, prosperous place, then shift to its building in 1648–1650 and the bloodshed, mischief-making, and power plays of that time, and then shift to the period 1840–1845 and the "taming" of the last Native Americans in the area, how the hacienda became a command post for Anglos who despised both the Spaniards in the house and the Native Americans outside. With the hacienda as a frame, the way to tell your story in a resonant way becomes clear to you.

Consider the case of the travel writer Paul Theroux. He had written two bestsellers about faraway places and was wondering what his next subject might be. American-born but living mainly in London, he realized one day that he didn't know England very well and that it might be interesting to train his eye on his adopted country. This is the vague idea stage: "Maybe I should do a book about England. But *what* about England?"

He started reading the existing travel literature about England, to become informed about his subject matter and to make sure that he didn't write a book that had already been written. What he realized immediately was that England is the most written-about country on the face of the earth. For a confident writer, this realization was not at all daunting but something of a tantalizing challenge. Theroux had his vague idea—to write some sort of commentary on the personality and peculiarities of England—but, to use his word, no *subject* yet. Here are his thoughts as he considered his book-idea-without-a-subject, as recounted in his introduction to *The Kingdom by the Sea.*

My route was crucial. It was the most important aspect of travel. In choosing a route, one was choosing a subject. But every mile of Britain had a road through it: there was a track across every field, a footpath in every acre of woods. Perhaps this was why I had never traveled in Britain: I had been unable to decide on the route.

And then I had my way: narrowly, around the entire coast.

It answered every need. There was only one coast, it was one undeviating route, and this way I would see the whole of Britain. In many respects, Britain was its coast—nowhere in Britain was more than sixty-five miles from the sea. Nearly the whole of the coast was unknown to me. And so as soon as I decided on this coastal route for my itinerary, I had my justification for the trip— the journey had the right shape; it had logic; it had a beginning and an end; and what better way was there to see an island than circumambulating its coast?

Exercise : MUTTERING

For the next day or two wander around the house (or the office, the supermarket, or wherever you find yourself) muttering "How shall my book be organized? How shall my book be organized?" Alternately, try muttering "What is my frame? What is my frame?" Carry a pad with you to jot down any ideas that arrive. When people stare at you strangely, smile.

EXTRACTING PRINCIPLES

When a new writing client comes to my office, I know nothing about what he or she wants to write except the headline I may have gotten when we set up the appointment. Clients want to know what they should bring with them when they come in, and my answer is always "you." All I need is the person and his or her brain. Then I begin, usually with a question like:

"What are you hoping to write?"

"Well," a new client will say, "I started out as a therapist with a general psychotherapy practice about a dozen years ago, but for the past several years I've started seeing lots of clients who are having trouble sleeping . . . plus I've had terrible insomnia myself . . . and I've really helped several of them . . . maybe even most of them . . . so I was thinking I would write about that—"

Because where we are going is almost certainly toward a self-help book, what is instantly front and center in my mind is the task of helping this client organize her thoughts and experiences in a way that makes sense for a self-help book. Her ultimate organizing frame is very likely to center on core principles—the seven steps of this, the nine secrets of that, the eight principles of the other—and so that is where I want to head immediately.

"What have you been calling it?" I proceed to ask.

"My book? *Aligned with the Night.* That's been my working title."

"Doesn't quite resonate. But we'll get to the title in a minute."

"I have lots to say about working with sleep problems but I haven't really focused on the title or how to organize the material—"

"Right. Let's do that now. Let's organize what you know in some rhetorically strong way."

"Meaning?"

"You know, the seven principles of this, the nine steps of that, the eleven secrets—"

"I like secrets! And seven is a magical number."

"Great! So we have the seven secrets of . . . of what?

"Well . . . what do you mean?"

"Literary agents like to call it 'the promise.'"

"Well, you sleep. 'Better sleep'?"

"Not bad. But 'great sleep' would excite us more."

"*The Seven Secrets of Great Sleep.* I love it."

"Good! So what are they? The secrets?"

"Well, there's always relaxation. I always help clients—"

"Great! That's one. Relaxation."

"There's always historical stuff, too. Stuff from the past that's keeping you awake."

"What to call that? In the same vein as 'relaxation.'"

"I don't know. Not 'historical analysis' . . ."

"Nope. Well, what's really going on? You want a person to relax and you want a person to . . . what? Exorcise the past? Cleanse—"

"No, I like that. Cleansing. Relaxation and Cleansing."

"Great! That's two."

"Then . . . well, I'm not sure how to say this. There's a spiritual component to sleeping well. But I don't know how to talk about it—"

"Okay. So there's relaxation, cleansing, and this spiritual component . . ."

"I can't seem to get it."

"It's only been two seconds! Relax, cleanse yourself—"

"Funny. Okay. Well . . . you need to relax, you need to cleanse yourself . . . you need to lighten up . . . which isn't the same thing as relaxing—"

"Is that a secret?"

"It is."

"Let's keep that, then. That's three."

"Right. So you need to relax, cleanse yourself, lighten up, and . . . darn! What to call this spiritual thing?"

"Well . . . let's try a few ideas. What about pray? As in praying leads to better health, some say?"

"That's interesting! But isn't that too . . . Judeo-Christian? It feels narrow."

"Maybe. Maybe not. It's probably a function of how you define 'pray,' how you use it, what you mean by it, and so forth. Maybe it's wrong, maybe it's right."

"Let's keep it for now. I like it pretty well! Relax, cleanse yourself, lighten up, pray. Okay!"

"Now for number five."

"I'm exhausted!"

"Not hardly. We can get to seven."

"You're tough! Okay. Let's see. There's general physical health."

"Get healthy."

"Fine. And . . . there's the interpersonal one. If you're sleeping with someone, how you're doing with that person. If you're sleeping alone, aloneness and loneliness, which are two different things—"

"How to say that one?"

"Mm—feels tough."

"This may not be what you had in mind, but what about 'love'?"

"Love? Love. No, that's interesting. Love as a verb. You need to love to get great sleep. I like it."

"That's six."

"And just the mechanics, a good bed, not missing your sleep point, those sorts of things—"

"Is that as big as the others?"

"It is. I've found—"

"Great. What to call it?"

"Something like 'prepare'? That isn't quite it. It's like having the basic tools and strategies . . . it's like both 'educate yourself' and 'arm yourself'—"

"That would put us at eight. Do you want to go with eight?"

"No. I like seven. I think we could put these two together as 'educate yourself,' that would be educate yourself about your best bed, your best bedtime, whether you're an owl or a lark, et cetera. I think that works."

"Let's see where we are. So it's: relax, cleanse yourself, lighten up, pray, get healthy, love, and educate yourself. You have a starting point."

"More than that!"

What I have just shown you is the idea of "extracting principles," and it extends to any nonfiction book you might be writing. Consider the following example. A photojournalist called me from New York. She had done the interesting thing of spending two years traveling with and photographing America's circuses. She had many excellent visual images and an academic publisher had expressed interest in publishing her book. What she needed now was a brief introduction to the photos. But she had spent months trying to write that brief introduction without getting much written.

She told me that she had tried to write about the circuses in a chronological way: "I met the Blini Brothers Circus on Tuesday and we traveled to Boise . . ." I said, "One, that would never make for a brief introduction, not if you attempted that with all the circuses, and two, it couldn't possibly do a meaningful job of communicating the big ideas from your adventure. The better way would be to organize the photos not chronologically or circus by circus but according to some number of themes that made sense to you, like 'sleaziness,' 'danger,' 'camaraderie,' 'showmanship,' 'boredom,' or whatever. Eight or ten categories. Then the intro would come."

It seemed to me that she had to step back, view her experiences from a distance, and make some important decisions about meaning. Extracting principles or themes from your material is one way to actively make meaning and to help yourself understand what your thoughts and experiences represent. This journalist had done the work of traveling with the circus, but understanding what she had learned from her travels was her new task.

Exercise : **EXTRACTING PRINCIPLES**

Think about your book idea. Get it in mind and let it settle down for a few seconds. Then see if you can "extract principles" from your material in the way that I extracted them in the preceding examples. You may want to set yourself a goal beforehand—say, that you are going to extract eight, ten, or twelve principles—and then change that number if you come up with many more or many fewer. The joy of arriving at a number like 10, say, is that, if those principles remain alive and smart to you after you reflect upon them, you have a good number around which to organize the chapters of your book.

FAST FRAMING AND SLOWER FRAMING

Thinking lazily about the cookbook you want to write, you might hear yourself say "I love to cook and I have some darned interesting recipes. But what is my cookbook *about*?" You know perfectly well—because you've learned to be truthful and frank with yourself—that a mere collection of your recipes is unlikely to interest an editor, since you're not a well-known chef or a celebrity of any sort. You realize that you must come up with an interesting frame if you are going to have any chance of selling your book.

So you continue musing. "Well, what are some of my favorite recipes? Let's see . . . I make a dandy sweet pickle relish . . . and a tangy cranberry relish . . . what about a relish book? Could be. But that's probably been done to death. We serve the cranberry relish at Thanksgiving . . . that is, in the fall . . . and I make my mint relish to serve with lamb . . . at Easter . . . I think I have a seasons kind of thing going here! The sweet pickle relish could go with barbecue, that'd be summer . . . so, what do I need? . . . I need a winter relish . . . why, there's my corn relish! We serve that with roasts! So I've got relishes . . . and seasons . . . it's just got to be *Great Relishes for Every Season.* If something like that doesn't already exist, I'm going to think about this very seriously."

Another would-be cookbook writer might not have a framing epiphany of this sort. Even though she had spent the past two years traveling in Provence, visiting with restaurant chefs and home chefs, and soaking up the atmosphere of southern France, no excellent organizational frame might have struck her yet. Of course, she could divide her book into appetizers, fish dishes, meat dishes, breads, and so on, but how boring such a frame would seem! No, she knows that she needs her own personal, idiosyncratic design. But that magical frame hasn't appeared yet. What can she do?

She can think about what ideas or principles she wants to share with readers. If she attempted this intellectual work, she might arrive at the following list:

- There's the matter of good technique. Even the average home chef in Provence can make a delicious, runny omelette, and virtually no one in America can. So I want to headline simple, important techniques that make all the difference, especially when it comes to two items many American visitors to France dream about when they get home: baguettes and croissants.

- I'd like to help readers learn how to find, choose, and use fresh, tasty ingredients. I had some extraordinary dishes made up of only a few essentials: maybe just green beans, heirloom tomatoes, salt, pepper, olive oil. But the green beans were delicious to start with, and so were the tomatoes, and that made all the difference. So I would have to research how the American home chef, wherever she lives, can get a tomato that tastes good. That makes me think that I want to use simplicity as an idea—gosh, the book could be called *Simply Provence* and focus on simple as a deep idea. I have to think about this.

- I'd also like the reader to enjoy the atmospherics of the south of France, the light that mesmerized the impressionist painters, how the mistral wind makes you want to prepare a hearty soup or stew, what associations old stone walls bring to mind.

- I'd also like to present dishes that are exciting, even *dangerous,* not dangerous in the sense that a flambé might set your curtains on fire but dangerous in the sense that a salty anchovy is really salty, that real saltiness feels dangerous to us in these days of tasteless food. I guess "bold flavors" is the phrase that's usually used in this context, but I'd like to frame it as a kind of danger to cook something that is really sour or really salty or so garlicky that your breath reeks for days.

- I'd also like a reader to come away loving this region—actually, I'd like a reader to come away loving food more. The book could even be called *In Love with Provence,* if that didn't seem too hokey. But something about love needs to permeate the book.

The first cookbook writer arrived at *Great Relishes for Every Season* in one fell swoop. The second cookbook writer hasn't arrived at her frame or her focus yet, but the work of extracting principles or themes can only prove beneficial to her. Her cookbook is unlikely to end up consisting of chapters with titles like "simplicity," "danger," and "love," and she may end up back at "appetizers," "fish dishes," and "breads." But in the journey back to that conventional place she will have learned what her book really wants to be about.

Chapter 4

THE ACTIVITY OF TITLING

I f you have been thinking about your nonfiction book, you have been thinking about how language operates, how words connote ideas and are related to ideas, how phrases are either richer or poorer in their resonant associations with ideas, and so on. Nowhere is this study more fruitful than in connection with the title and subtitle of your book.

These two elements of your nonfiction book are very important, because they have the job of communicating information to readers (including editors and agents) and, just as important, because they hold the meaning of your book for you as you write it. They are the banner headlines for your book, and if they effectively communicate what your book intends to be, they help you stay on track.

When you arrive at a useful title and a subtitle, you know what your book is about and you continue to know it until you complete your project (unless, during the actually writing, your book morphs and becomes another book). You will have only a fuzzy idea of what you are writing about if you think of your book as "something about ocean rowing and spirituality." But you will have a very clear idea—and therefore better motivation and better chances of success—if you have arrived at *Rowing Toward God: The Seven Principles of Sacred Rowing*. Possessing this title and subtitle means that you have your frame and your focus in place; they then serve as excellent reminders of how you will organize your material.

Once you have a good idea of what your book intends to be about, actively working to arrive at a title and a subtitle are excellent next steps that can further clarify your book's focus. If you do not have your focused book idea yet, thinking about titles and subtitles, playing with them, and brainstorming many alternatives will help you arrive at that idea. Your title and subtitle complement and support each other and provide you and readers with a clarity that a title alone is less able to provide, so your goal is to produce two strong, related phrases that together effectively and beautifully describe your book's intention and that work to excite a reader's mind.

Unfortunately, certain psychological mechanisms come into play that regularly prevent writers from thinking clearly about the title and subtitle of their book. Because they are afraid that they will not select well, because they mistake a lack of clarity for subtlety and a prideful refusal to communicate for literary license, because they are secretly at war with agents and editors and do not want to give them what they need, and for many other, similarly unfortunate reasons, writers often paste a boring, unclear title onto their book, skip the subtitle altogether, and call themselves done. This happens so often that it appears almost to be the rule rather than the exception.

For example, a student in one of my book proposal writing classes refused to brainstorm a list of potential subtitles for her memoir. Instead, she provided me with a list of 33 memoirs that did not come with subtitles, among them *A Backward Glance, The Same River Twice, Rain or Shine, Facts of Life, Stop Time, The Gift,* and *Fierce Attachments.* She also did not agree that a title needed to impart any information. To prove her point, she also supplied me with a list of 10 titles of books by the well-known nonfiction author John McPhee, including *The Deltoid Pumpkin Seed, Pieces of the Frame, In Suspect Terrain, Levels of the Game, Coming into the Country,* and *Assembling California.* But her lists only proved that some published authors are not interested in providing information to their readers via their titles and that some editors occasionally allow or even champion noninformative titles and sometimes consider subtitles unnecessary.

Just as would-be authors often object to creating a lively and informative title and a subtitle for their book, they also often object to letting go of the first title that pops into their head. However, this first title may turn out to be inappropriate, and it is dangerous to fall in love with it. It is one thing if your title doesn't help readers identify with your subject, but it is a graver matter if you choose a working title that prevents you from writing the right book. The real danger of adamantly hanging on to a working title is that the act of hanging on locks you into the first version of your book, and the first version may be very different from the one you ultimately want to write.

For example, you might start out thinking that your book is about creativity in business. The title *Beethoven in the Boardroom* pops into your head and you fall in love with it. But as you write, you discover that your book is more about building employee self-confidence than creativity at work. Either your working title actually impedes your progress on the book or, if you proceed to write about building employee self-confidence, causes a distracting disconnect between what is in the book and what a person picking it up might reasonably expect to find inside. If the conflict grows too great between hanging on to your original idea, as marked by your first title, and letting the book grow as it wants to, you will stall and feel blocked.

An excellent way to handle these problems is to brainstorm many titles and subtitles. The activity of brainstorming titles unpacks your vague idea, if it is still vague, and lays out the many possibilities embedded in it. If your idea is already focused, brainstorming titles helps you arrive at precise representations of the meaning you intend to make in resonant language that will intrigue agents, editors, and readers. It also forces you to let go of the idea that there is only one possible title for your book and puts you in the habit of constructing titles that are very practical, very literary, and everything in between. The activity of titling can be so powerful an exercise that sometimes you can move from the vague idea stage to the focused idea stage in a split second, just by landing on the perfect, resonant title.

Exercise : BRAINSTORM TITLES

Dream up 10, 20, 30, or more potential titles for your book. Write them all down. Do not censor yourself or secretly aim your mind in the direction of a title you already harbor as the "right one." Brainstorm titles that connect in any way whatsoever to your book idea, keeping in mind that your only goal is to **put down anything and everything.**

Exercise : A TITLE AND ALTERNATIVES

If you've had a book title in mind for a long time or one title has risen to the top of the list you generated in the previous exercise, write down this "first place" title at a top of a fresh sheet of paper. Without referring back to the list you just brainstormed, create a dozen alternative titles to your "first place" title.

Exercise : A SUBTITLE AND ALTERNATIVES

Do the same work with respect to your subtitle. First, brainstorm 10, 20, or 30 possible subtitles for your book. Then choose your favorite subtitle from the list and let it head a new sheet of paper. Next brainstorm a dozen alternatives.

At the end of these exercises you may or may not have a title and a subtitle in place, but you will have done excellent work exploring your idea.

As you work on titling your book, consider using the idioms and cultural conventions of your native language as a kind of shorthand to help you succinctly capture the concept and nuances of the idea you're writing about. Consider the common phrase "new and improved." Say that you are writing a book in which you mean to argue that progress is overrated. As you think about your book, it occurs to you that the phrase "new and improved" represents everything you dislike about contemporary culture. It also strikes you that that very phrase, or some variation, might be used as your book's title.

One possible title might be *New and Unimproved: Unmasking the Myth of Progress.* A second possible title might be *Have We Really Improved? Why the Old Ways Are the Better Ways.* A third possible title might be *New and Improved: What Advertisers Want You to Believe.* By using this well-known expression or some variation on it, you make use of the built-in resonances that a phrase like "new and improved" carries in our society.

A word or phrase may work in your title because it has a useful homonym. Say that you are a university professor contemplating writing a book about critical thinking skills geared to a general audience. You want to clarify terms like *analysis, synthesis,* and *evaluation* in a breezy way, demonstrating how to counter any argument by mimicking the form of that argument, explaining why word-of-mouth recommendations carry disproportionate weight, and so on. You want a title that captures a sense of the breeziness you are aiming at and one day the title *Thinking Aloud* pops into your head. You like it a lot, but you are also aware that it has some extra resonance that also pleases you: *Thinking Aloud* suggests to readers that it is permissible to think, as in *Thinking Allowed.*

You might be able to combine the cultural associations of a phrase like "new and improved" with the way homonyms add depth, as with "aloud" and "allowed," as in the following example. Say that you are a Japanese-American woman writing a memoir about your secret love affair with an African-American man. One day the title for your memoir strikes you: *A Taste for Spinach.* You have to smile, because your English-speaking audience will not understand that title until you explain it.

In English there is no linguistic association between *spinach* and *secret love* but in Japanese the word for *spinach* is a homonym for the word for *secret love.* For hundreds of years in Japan, the way to show your devotion to your secret lover was to give him or her a present in a spinach-green bag. Not only does your title provide resonances for a Japanese speaker and mysterious overtones for an English speaker, but suddenly you see that the metaphor of "gifts" can be used thematically throughout your memoir.

Sometimes the hunt for just the right word or phrase for your title leads you to large, unexpected problems that are better faced at the beginning of your project than a year later. Say, for example, you intend to write about a particular aspect of psychological denial that interests you, namely those cases where people are in denial about one or two things but are not otherwise defensive. You rack your brain trying to think of what word or phrase will capture your idea. Then one day the answer strikes you. You realize that the phrase has been there all along and that Carl Jung coined it: blind spot. It is disappointing that Jung got there first and that a whole body of literature on the subject exists already. But the activity of titling alerted you to this fact early enough that you can decide what you want to do before you've invested a lot of time in the project.

Once you understand how language can be used to express—and to sell—ideas, you will do a better job of presenting your focused book idea in a way that interests readers. Say that you are contemplating writing a self-help book for fearful transvestites. The title *Everything You Ever Wanted to Know About Cross-Dressing but Were Afraid to Ask* pops into your head. Your first reaction is to suppose that such a title promises too much. Upon reflection, though, you realize that no reader who understands the conventions of our society would be misled. We all know that your book intends to tell us a lot about cross-dressing but not really everything.

The same is true for titles like *The Seven Principles of Home Beekeeping* (of course there aren't only or exactly seven principles, but presumably we are going to be taught seven useful and important principles), *Atomic Physics Made Easy* (of course it will never really be easy to understand, but by the end of our reading we ought to have a better idea of the basics), or *The Last Guide to Retirement You Will Ever Need* (of course we will need an updated version if Social Security goes bankrupt or if the federal government authorizes a new sort of IRA). These hyperbolic titles are not misleading because we understand them perfectly.

However, because language is powerful and because power can be a corrupting influence, a danger exists that we will choose resonant linguistic phrases in order to seduce and mislead potential readers. *A History of God,* for example, is not a history of God but a history of religious thought. But which book are believers in monotheism more likely to buy—*A History of God,* which implies that God exists and is a unity, or *A History of Religious Thought,* which brings to mind division rather than unity and doubt rather than surety? *A History of God* is a seductive title that, if we drew a line in the sand, is perhaps just on the legitimate side, since a prospective reader should probably recognize what such a book would actually be about. But it is very close to the line.

Over the line is *The Math Gene.* The author of *The Math Gene* begins his narrative by telling his readers that there is no math gene. Why does his title say one thing and his text another? Because no one will buy a book with the title "math ability is a natural human phenomenon"—the actual thesis of his book—but many people will buy a book that looks like it will explain why they were never good at math: "See, Dorothy, I just don't have the math gene!" If you were to buy this book on the basis of its title alone, I think you would expect to learn that there is a math gene, or, at the very least, that the hunt is on for one and that the prospects of finding it look promising. If you opened *The Math Gene* and read first thing that there was no such thing as a math gene, I think you would feel misled.

TWENTY-FIVE FRAMES

Say that you are a motivational speaker and you know you want to write a book about building confidence. You have the hunch that "confidence" or some variant like "confident" ought to find its way into your title. One way to brainstorm a large number of titles is to make use of the list of 25 "frames" that appear next. Each of these is a general selling point. You can play around with potential titles for your book that suggest how your idea will offer each of these sales and marketing benefits. For your book on confidence, you might generate the following list of titles:

1. Newness: *Brand New Confidence!*
2. Simplification: *Confidence for Dummies*
3. Ease: *Grow Confident While You Nap!*
4. Comprehensiveness: *Total Confidence*
5. Demystification: *Secrets of the Confident Person*
6. Increases: *Triple Your Confidence*
7. Connecting *x* with *y*: *The Zen of Confidence*
8. Personal creativity: *The Art of Confidence*
9. Mood management: *Beat the Blues by Becoming Confident*
10. Life span vitality: *Lifelong Confidence*
11. Psychological health and healing: *Confidence Is the Cure!*
12. Specific psychological disorders: *More Confidence, Less Anxiety!*
13. Mind/body integration: *Confident Mind, Confident Body*
14. Spirituality: *The Soul of Confidence*
15. Personal effectiveness: *Take Charge Confidently!*
16. Time management: *One Hour to Greater Confidence*
17. Relationship management: *Network with Confidence*
18. Community building: *The Confident Organization*
19. Value building: *Confidence Is a Virtue!*
20. Confidence building: *Five Steps to Perfect Confidence*
21. Rootedness: *Coming Home to Your Confident Self*
22. Process: *The Eight Stages of Confidence Building*

23. Strategies: *The Seven Habits of Confident People*
24. Categories: *Confidence Breeds Winners*
25. Alternative Approaches: *Thirty Wild Ways to Increase Your Confidence*

While most of these titles aren't great, several are pretty good. A few might be close to what you had in mind and were hunting for all along. *Total Confidence* might alert you to the idea that a person could be taught how to become more confident across the board, in everything that he or she attempted in life. *One Hour to Greater Confidence* might get you thinking about how people could be helped to grow more confident quickly. *Confident Mind, Confident Body* might connect to ideas you've harbored for some time about how growing more confident increases a person's overall fitness and health.

You can use these frames to help you think about any sort of nonfiction book. Your book on cooking with herbs can be about "new herb recipes," "easy herb recipes," "the seven secrets of cooking with herbs," or "herbs that heal." Your biography of Marx can be a new look at Marx, a comprehensive look at Marx, an examination of Marx's seven most important ideas, or a book about "real Marxists" versus "false Marxists." Your memoir can be about your life over time (a lifespan book), as it relates to a certain physical place (engaging with the idea of rootedness), or as process (as in the idea of stages of one's life).

Exercise : **TWENTY-FIVE FRAMES**

First, identify a key word or words that you believe will appear in your title, like "ocean rowing," "confidence," or "herbs." Next, use the 25 frames just listed to create 25 titles for your book that sound like the titles of books you'd see in your local bookstore.

If you aren't positive about your key word—say, if you aren't sure whether your book about early Communists will have Marx, Engels, or Trotsky in the title, or all three—repeat the exercise until you've tried every variation. Similarly, if you have alternate key words—say, if you aren't sure whether you are promoting "growth," "healing," or "change" in your book on confidence—repeat the exercise using each alternative key word.

Exercise : CREATE YOUR OWN FRAMES

An extension of this exercise is to create your own list of frames. Can you think of other sales-and-marketing "angles" or other rhetorical frames to add to my list of 25? A cookbook writer, for example, might add a frame like "authentic" to her list. A travel writer might add frames like "hidden" and "untouched" to his list. Add some of your own frames to my list or create your own unique list of frames. You can use your personalized list of frames for the book you are currently writing and for future books, too.

GETTING OUT OF YOUR OWN WAY

There are writers who can organize, plan, and write good work for hire but who feel blocked when it comes to tackling their own book. They can create a sixty-thousand-word manual in two months but can't squeeze out seven words on the book they have been meaning to write for a decade. How strange this is! These writers already have experienced the process: they know what it takes to make a book. They know how to think. They know how to organize. They know how to plan. They know how the spellcheck on their computer works and how to move paragraphs around. They know how to revise and work with editorial feedback. They know everything under the sun. What's going on?

I think the answer is that as soon as we say to ourselves "I would like to do some work that really matters," we scare ourselves half to death. We have suddenly raised the stakes to a terrifying height, by demanding that we do excellent work and make some important meaning. We do not want to put ourselves in a position where we might make a terrible mess, fail, and end up calling ourselves bad names. Of course, retreating from our work causes us to call ourselves exactly those bad names, so we haven't really spared our ego anything. The risk of going forward, however, feels like the graver risk.

This is why, for many people, the point of having arrived at a good idea, a good title, and a good organizational scheme is a crucial one fraught with pitfalls. You may find yourself stopped dead in your tracks just at the moment when you would suppose that you'd be eager to begin writing your book. Take the following example. I had been working with a client who had arrived at a good idea for a book on sleepwalking. I had asked him to produce a query letter as an exercise, and then I suggested that he send it out to a few literary agents. I wanted to gauge his reaction to my request, as I had the feeling that he was at that critical point of being particularly vulnerable to anxiety and self-doubt. This was his response.

Dear Eric:

I didn't realize we were really going to send this in! What happens when (or if) I actually have to write the damn book? I'm making this up as I go along. There might not even be a book here. And I don't know anything really about the subject other than glancing at a few articles on the Internet. Wasn't this just an "exercise"? Even if I could actually write the thing (and I'm not sure even how to do research for any of the chapters!) what if these people did call me up and ask me about the book and since I don't know anything really about the subject, what would I say? And then I'm not even sure this is something I want to write (or are you saying that doesn't matter?) and spend a year or so of my time trying to learn about something I'm not sure I even care about (or are you saying that too doesn't matter?).

This would-be nonfiction writer suddenly felt completely unequal to the task. Objectively, nothing had happened from one moment to the next except that producing his book had become something more of a reality. But this was enough to cause him to panic. Will you panic and throw up psychological obstacles to getting on with your task when you get to this point? It's certainly possible. One way to handle any psychological obstacles that may arise is to prepare yourself beforehand. The following exercise will help you with these preparations.

Exercise : **GETTING OUT OF YOUR OWN WAY**

Identify some of the obstacles that you might have a tendency to put in your own way—for example, negative self-talk, an inability to tolerate the anxiety of the unknown, the worry that you have no talent—as you embark on your book. Spend an hour or so naming a few of these obstacles and becoming familiar with them. Now try to think of some things that you might do—at least one thing per challenge—that will help you deal with these obstacles. Describe what you will do to survive and overcome them (like crafting and using affirmations, learning techniques from cognitive therapy such as thought blocking and thought substitution, etc.).

THE TIME TO BEGIN WRITING

You have done a lot of thinking and note-taking so far. When is it time to begin writing? The following four scenarios give examples of writers with very different projects and personalities working under very different circumstances. Let's look at how the time to begin writing is unique for each.

1. Jane has a focused book idea in mind: "a book about stress management organized around the nine principles that I teach in my seminars for firefighters and directed specifically to the concerns of firefighters." She rightly recognizes that such a book, were she to write it, would earn her additional income at her seminars and attract new business. But Jane also has a second focused idea in mind, one that interests her considerably more than the first: "a book about stress management organized around the nine principles that I teach in my seminars for firefighters, but directed to women and more philosophical in tone than my firefighter book would be."

In order to arrive at the time to begin writing, Jane's task is to choose. Since she feels relatively sure that she is organizing her book around the nine principles she teaches, whichever version she writes, the key to beginning is to make a tentative but nevertheless whole-hearted commitment to one version. Until she chooses, she is likely to feel blocked and stymied. Once she chooses, she can begin to write, reflect on what she's written, and either recommit to her first choice or change her mind and start on her second choice.

2. Bill has one book idea that feels like his first choice and several alternative ideas. His focused idea is "to write a self-help book for people addicted to Internet gambling, describing in the first part, through statistics and vignettes, the extent of the problem, explaining in the sec-

ond part the root causes of addiction to Internet gambling, and providing in the third part a complete program for ending an Internet gambling addiction." His alternative ideas are "to cover all forms of gambling, using the same format," "to take a historical approach and look at gambling addictions throughout history," and "to focus on the stories of five or six Internet gambling addicts, telling each of their stories in a chapter and finishing up with self-help strategies."

Although he isn't positive that his first choice will remain his first choice, he recognizes that he is at a point where doing some writing feels like the appropriate next step. Rather than completely outline book 1, which may not be the book he will ultimately write, he decides to try his hand at articulating what he believes are the root causes of gambling addictions. He knows that, no matter which of these books he chooses to write, he will need to be able to express his thoughts clearly about the causes of a gambling addiction, so it can only prove beneficial to get started writing about that.

3. Mary, who wants to write about her schizophrenic brother, has no clear idea what form her book should take, what it should cover, or what she intends to say. None of the exercises she tried clarified her idea or her intention, and whether she didn't fully engage with them or whether they weren't right for her is now beside the point. She has the feeling that what she must do next is write, not knowing where she is going or what she intends to say.

But she has taken to heart my warning that "just writing" isn't the best idea and pledges to herself that after four weeks of writing she will stop and assess her progress. Because she is framing these four weeks as a time for exploration, not for "getting things right," and because she knows that in a month she will have the opportunity to pause and reflect, she finds herself ready to encounter the blank screen of her computer.

4. Mark has only a title, *Secret Recipes from the Deep South,* and a vague idea of what he wants to include in his book. But he has the strong sense that his title is rich and resonant enough that if he keeps it in mind he will find his way. He concludes that his next best step is to begin writing. He decides to start on the book's introduction, to learn more about what his book intends to contain by wrestling an introduction into existence. He recognizes that, if his efforts to write the introduction do not prove fruitful, he may have to think about his book idea again or choose another section of his book to write. But for now embarking on the introduction feels like the right approach.

Each of these writers has arrived at a different point. But each has done sufficient work that writing is the next logical step. You, too, may have arrived at this point, and writing may be the next logical step for you. As you write, you may find that you are thrown into confusion, wonder if you know enough to write your book, suspect that one of your other book ideas might be a wiser one to pursue, and otherwise doubt that you are ready to write. All of this confusion is natural, perhaps even inevitable. However, you don't want to let your fear and anxiety about what may be ahead of you prevent you from beginning. If writing is the next reasonable thing for you to do, it is time to begin the adventure of diving into your material and organizing your thoughts on paper.

CHUNKING

Now that you're ready to write, I'd like you to do so.

I'd like you to begin by writing what I call chunks. A chunk is a piece of writing about the length of a newspaper column that, like a newspaper column, treats a single subject in a rounded, complete, self-contained way. In your book it might be an anecdote, a vignette, an exercise, a complete thought, a description of a place or an event. As you get practiced at writing nonfiction you will acquire an increasingly fine sense of what chunks feel like and what they can accomplish. Chunks are the building blocks of nonfiction books.

In this chapter you'll be writing five chunks of your book. The first step in deciding which chunks to write is an emotional one: to make a commitment to one version of your book. It is actually a tentative commitment, which sounds like an oxymoron because it is shorthand for the following idea. You are to make a *full* commitment to one version of your book, while reserving the right to change your mind after you've done some writing. It is like committing to your marriage but reserving the right to get a divorce if your mate turns out to be an ax murderer or a philanderer. As long as your mate is an appropriate mate, you are committed and will not philander yourself or divorce him because of a bad hair day. But should he fail to uphold his end of the marital bargain in some big way, you are out of there.

Which version of your book will you choose? Consider the following scenario. A writer we'll call Jim is interested in exploring how actors in regional theater manage to make a living. He has many ideas about the craft of acting and the lives of actors and envisions his book as an interview book with his brief commentary supplementing the interviews. He's thought of *Caught in the Act* for his book's title and *Interviews with the Best Actors You'll Never Know* as its subtitle. But he knows that his job is to think clearly about his book and not to fall in love with a particular title, subtitle, or organizational scheme.

If he were to craft a book based on the idea, title, and subtitle he's created, he would end up conducting interviews with local actors, interviews that might be far-ranging and quite interesting. But three large problems would rise up to confront him. First, he would end up with an ordinary interview book, which probably would be very hard to market. Second, he would have failed to craft personal meaning, relying instead on the meaning his interviewees contributed. Third, he might have trouble producing a book that matched his original impulse, because his subjects would probably want to talk about what was important to them, not necessarily what was important to him.

Thinking about these things, it strikes Jim that it would be interesting to try to identify some principles or qualities that thriving regional actors have in common. Out of the blue, he is reminded of something he read somewhere, that actors have to be as crafty as rats to find work and earn a living. In the next instant he remembers a quote from the French actress Arletty: "I am the cat that walks alone." The proverbial light bulb goes on, and he is struck by the idea of relating actors' professional survival skills to the identifying characteristics of certain animals. This is a moment of inspiration that only comes because he has been holding the intention to write his book and because he has paused with his whole being to think about his book. He opens his pad and begins to jot down notes:

Elephant: *thick hide, metaphor for being able to take rejection, criticism, direction, etc.*

Rat: *crafty, will do anything to survive.*

Cat: *walks alone, but also grooms other cats, not a pack or herd animal but strategically sociable.*

Eagle: *pride, idea of taking pride in whatever you do, small or large, and also thinking big, soaring high, there are no small actors, only small roles, etc.*

Chameleon: *although acting is revelation, disguise and shape-shifting are important, and also adapting to different environments, tough here, gentle there, working with different directors, different ensembles, etc.*

Camel: *going without water, inner resources, stamina, hard work of the run of the play plus maybe also the hard work of a day job, and also going without, sacrificing, doing with less, chronic unemployment.*

Just like that a title comes to him: *Elephant and Rat: The Six Survival Skills of the Working Actor.*

After a few seconds of intense excitement, Jim's enthusiasm wanes.

First, his book has now become not an interview book but one he will actually have to write. He hadn't really pictured himself writing a book but rather cobbling a book together from interviews he would conduct. The task of actually writing a book suddenly feels burdensome and daunting. Does he have a book in him? Does he have enough to say? Has he the credentials to present himself as an expert on actors' survival skills? Jim wonders if this "good" idea wasn't planted in his brain by some trickster.

Second, he is several animals short. Six animals feel like too few. No book has just six chapters. Should he go with these six, struggle to think up a seventh, an eighth, and a ninth, or do some other work on the book while more animals come to him? Instead of feeling proud and happy that six animals have already come to him, Jim feels dismayed and disappointed that more haven't arrived. Fortunately, he determines to take a deep breath, step back, and not allow himself to become pessimistic.

He decides to wait and see how many more animals want to come forward. Until that happens, he can just work on writing parts of his book. Released from needing to know how many animals his book will contain, he finds himself excited again. He loves how these animals can be used to stand for important concepts, and he recognizes that the excitement he feels may also be felt by agents and editors.

But what should he do next? Should he begin to conduct interviews with local working actors, which, first of all, would mean getting some interview questions in order? Should he reread some of the acting interview books already out there, to see what actors have said about his six principles? Something tells him that both possibilities are off base and that his job is to stop and do more thinking.

The next question he asks himself is particularly fruitful: if he were to write some chunks of *Elephant and Rat,* which would be the most logical chunks to write? It seems too soon to start on an introduction: he doesn't really know enough about the book yet. Nor does he have any idea how the chapters will be designed or what they will contain. Originally primarily an interview book, his project is now a book that, enriched by material from the interviews he conducts, he will have to think into existence. What *will* the chapters contain?

Pondering this question, he has the following conversation with himself:

"Well, each chapter will need an introduction, where I describe a specific skill or principle and talk about it a bit. That's pretty clear. Then . . . I can see something like a bulleted list, like 'ten ways to grow the hide of an elephant.' Then . . . what? Well, maybe a story where not having a tough hide hurt an actor and where having that kind of hide helps. But I can't write those stories until I conduct my interviews . . . unless . . . unless I make them up. Maybe I'm going to want to create vignettes based on what I already know about actors, and not hope that interviewees will feed me what I need. In that case . . . wow . . . do I even need to conduct interviews? Can I make it up out of whole cloth, right out of my head? I have to think about that. Then . . . what else? Maybe an exercise that helps build a thick skin. Then maybe . . . common situations that test the thickness of your skin, like auditions, trying to get an agent, working with a nasty director, working with stars with big egos, et cetera. Then . . . no, I'd really like some first-person accounts from actors that I know, so maybe not exactly interviews but some solicited pieces . . . I could ask Barry to contribute on this point, he's got the most amazing way of handling criticism and rejection . . . so maybe a couple of solicited pieces in each chapter . . . maybe even a few from celebrities, if I could get those . . . if I wanted those . . . I'm not sure. At any rate . . . maybe I have a plan. I think I see what each chapter would look like."

Jim has just produced a template for his chapters, a model of how each chapter will look and what each chapter will contain. This is an excellent accomplishment and very important to the life of his book.

He decides to choose the elephant chapter to work on and further decides to write five chunks for that chapter that fit his model. Over the next several days he writes the chapter introduction, which forces him to understand the principle he's examining and the very idea of a principle. He tries his hand at a vignette, which provides him with the interesting experience of writing "fiction" or "creative nonfiction." He writes a chunk about situations requiring a thick skin, which turns out to be an extended list, then a skin-thickening exercise, which becomes a fourth chunk, and then the chapter's conclusion, which gives him a sense of how each chapter will connect with the next and what summing up the chapter sounds like.

When he's done he has 20 pages written, a significant portion of this chapter. He is also convinced that he has chosen an organizational scheme that has good metaphoric resonance and that will allow him to make full use of what he knows about his topic. In the space of a few days he has gone from "writing an interview book" to having a solid, resonant book idea and much of a sample chapter written.

CHUNKING A MEMOIR

Let's say that you're writing a book that does not lend itself to the idea of model chapters, as Jim's book on actors did. What chunks will you tackle in that set of circumstances? Consider the case of Sheila, who completes the exercise on page 58 in the following way.

Ten Things I'm Providing to Readers

1. Information on brain tumors and what it looks like when one person slowly loses various faculties, one by one.

2. The wild range of emotions and thoughts family members experience during this time, humor and pathos, lust and love, hate and frustration, acceptance and anxiety, laughter in the midst of horror. Fighting and love are NOT OPPOSITE.

3. Reflections on the role of music in our lives and deaths.

4. The way light and sight inform our lives and deaths.

5. Evocative descriptions of Lake Superior, Marin Headland, and Duluth.

6. Laughs.

7. Understanding how one large family deals with the crisis of a sibling dying at home, the differences in the ways people react to difficult situations, what is different about large families. How two different parental cultures, Jewish and Catholic, influence the way a family operates.

8. An intimate view of a relationship between two emotionally ambivalent sisters at a time when one is dying. What in the past contributed to how they are now? How they define themselves against each other. How the older sister cares for the younger sister. A look at both of their feelings of inadequacy in life, love, and caretaking.

9. Provides the reader who may be going through such a difficult experience with less isolation, less aloneness in her feelings of anger, frustration, absurdity, and silliness during a difficult time.

10. Me and my sensibility: my attempt to tell my feelings and how I try to understand this particular ambivalent relationship.

A smart way for Sheila to choose which chunks of her memoir to write would be for her to look at her list of "ten things I'm providing readers" and say to herself, "Which five of these do I want to write about?" If she did this, she might engage in the following inner dialogue:

"I could do a chunk on what a brain tumor is and what it's like to lose your mental faculties. Would that be a 'scientific' piece or a personal piece? I'm not sure. Let me think about that. I probably should do a chunk on the 'wild range of emotions' theme, since that's so central to the book. But what does that actually mean? Probably I should get a concrete instance in mind where Julie was up one minute and down the next, or maybe where I was hopeful one minute and devastated the next. That chunk almost *has* to be written, since it is so representative of the book's center. If I can't handle writing that, I may have real trouble writing the book at all.

"Three and four feel hard: would I do a chunk on the role of music, or how the quality of light defines a place? Maybe I should do 'light' as part of five—maybe I should try my hand at one evocative description, maybe of Lake Superior. Could I get the music theme in there? Possibly. That feels valuable to do, since I want a rich sense of setting throughout the book. So that will be the second chunk: an evocative description of Lake Superior, laced somehow with the meaning thread of a dying sister and a terrible, tumultuous time, and also light and music.

"Now, let's see, six, what I'm calling 'laughs.' Not sure. Let's peek at seven. Well, I certainly have to do a chunk out of seven, how the family dealt with all of this, but what moment should I choose? I say that I want to deal with two parental cultures, Jewish and Catholic. Can I find a moment or a scene that captures that dynamic? I think so. I think the moment when Rose tries to wax philosophical about death and Mary breaks down and screams at her, I think that captures something about the two cultures. I should try to write that scene.

"And eight—that's also central to the book. 'How they define themselves against each other.' What do I mean by that? Is there some event that shows that? It could be the day Julie and I went shopping, how we got into that fight about that short skirt . . . no, that feels clichéd somehow. I'll have to think about that. So . . . nine . . . that's the self-help aspect of the book. Do I really mean to include any of that? Maybe trying a chunk of that would help me know if I have it in me to sound like an expert and offer some advice. That feels challenging, but maybe it's smart to try. So . . . I think that's it. My five chunks are: (1) Emotional roller coaster chunk, (2) Evocative description of Lake Superior chunk, (3) Family chunk with a strong focus on Catholic/Jewish differences, (4) A chunk about how Julie and I defined ourselves against each other, and (5) Something like advice chunk."

The process for choosing which chunks to write is the same irrespective of the sort of book you're writing. It is the same process whether you have a solid idea about your book's central meaning and organizational scheme or only a vague idea. The process is to stop and honestly appraise what you know about your book at this precise moment, as Jim and Sheila did. You accept any anxiety that arises as you do the work of choosing, remembering that choosing almost always provokes anxiety. You catch your breath and try as best as you can to decide which chunks would be important and useful to write at this stage of the process.

Exercise : **CHOOSING YOUR CHUNKS**

Choose five chunks of your book that you mean to write and give each one a headline name, like "the scene between Alphonse and Gaston" or "the first insomnia checklist." Then try to articulate why you've chosen these chunks to write. You might use the following format:

Chunk 1. Name:

I am choosing this chunk to write because:

Chunk 2. Name:

I am choosing this chunk to write because:

Chunk 3. Name:

I am choosing this chunk to write because:

Chunk 4. Name:

I am choosing this chunk to write because:

Chunk 5. Name:

I am choosing this chunk to write because:

Exercise : WRITING AND EVALUATING
YOUR CHUNKS

Write your five chunks. Then reread each one. Try to be evaluative rather than critical. You might use the following format to evaluate your chunks.

Chunk 1. Name:

My thoughts about Chunk 1:

Chunk 2. Name:

My thoughts about Chunk 2:

Chunk 3. Name:

My thoughts about Chunk 3:

Chunk 4. Name:

My thoughts about Chunk 4:

Chunk 5. Name:

My thoughts about Chunk 5:

Next, try to articulate your improved understanding of your book.

1. I would now articulate my book's central idea as:
2. I see that I may have to let go of my desire to:
3. I believe that its organizational scheme will be:
4. I believe that it ought to be more (or less) secularized because:
5. I would now identify its meaning thread as:
6. I believe that its title now is:
7. I believe that its subtitle now is:

HAVING CHUNKED

If your chunks please you and confirm that you have envisioned your book correctly, congratulations! Your next steps are to continue writing more chunks in the same strategic, thoughtful way and then to begin to put together your book proposal (which I will discuss in the next chapter). If, however, you feel sad, bewildered, and daunted by your chunks rather than pleased by them, you may be processing the fact that actually writing your book tests your ideas and your courage in ways that no amount of preparation can prevent. This is a moment when many writers, unhappy with what they're writing and with how little they're writing, may leap to the notion that they have no talent, that they don't know enough, and that they're too mush-brained and easily distractible to concentrate.

What they need is a fairy godmother to whisper, "You are just *beginning,* you are in the unknown territory that every writer must traverse, this is not about you but about the *process,* you are like every soldier finally facing the enemy. This is scary and hard but *entirely normal* and your only job is to persevere. Write, discard, write, discard—surrender to the process and do not give up!"

This is a great moment of truth in the writing process, writing your first chunks. Suddenly your idiosyncratic grammar problems rise up to haunt you. Every sentence may sound a little bit off—too stiff, too breezy, too convoluted, less interesting by a mile than you had hoped, off on tangents you had no intention of pursuing, muddy, confused, dead, unbeautiful.

This is no problem! The only problem is that you are extrapolating from the truth of the matter—that your first sentences, paragraphs, and chunks don't work yet—an indictment about you as a writer and a thinker. Do not fall back in self-loathing and fear! Instead, return to your computer and revise this chunk or that chunk or write a new one. Write and think, write and think.

The problems you are experiencing are likely to fall into two very different categories: how poorly you are writing, on the one hand, and your book wanting to change its shape as you come to understand it better, on the other. The first problem you can cure by rewriting. The second problem you cure by revisioning your book. Neither is work for the faint of heart, but the second requires extra courage. Do not despair and do not doubt that you are equal to the task. Just say, gently but bravely, "I had an idea for a book and now I have some actual chunks written. Is my idea still valid and viable? Where exactly am I?"

You may learn that your book was incorrectly framed. Maybe another frame has already come forward as the more appropriate or compelling one. Maybe Jim's animal scheme didn't seem so viable in the actual writing and now sticking with the principles but dropping the animals makes more sense to him. Sheila may learn that her book is not so much about her relationship with her dying sister but more about the dynamics of her extended family. Conversely, she may learn that the meaning thread of her book is entirely the relationship between herself and her sister, and that a sharp focus needs to be maintained, forcing the exclusion of a lot of material that she had been sure would find its way into the book. Although it's disconcerting and disappointing to make these discoveries, the good news is that in doing so you will have gotten that much closer to framing your book correctly.

Exercise : NEXT CHUNKS

Having written five chunks and reevaluated the shape and purpose of your book, your next task is to continue writing chunks and learning more about your book. Think about where you actually want to go next in the unfolding of your book and try to name the chunks you next mean to write. This naming might sound like the following:

- "I am ready to write chapter 3 all the way through from beginning to end."
- "I think that I know enough about my book to try my hand at the introduction."
- "I think I understand most of the principles I'm writing about, but I'm not sure I understand the seventh one. I had better try to write something on that one, just to make sure it holds water."
- "It's still not clear to me if my memoir is about my early years in Tucson or my later adventures in California. What chunks could I choose to write that would help me clarify my intentions?"
- "I think I understand how my chapter model works, but the self-help exercise I created doesn't sound effective or convincing. Maybe I should write three or four more exercises, to learn how to make them work."
- "I think I can envision all of my chapters except the second and the sixth. I'd better choose one or the other of those to do a little writing in."

- "I think I understand my book in a way that allows me to go forward linearly, doing chapter 1 first, then chapter 2, and so on."

Exercise : PLANNING A MONTH OF WRITING

After you've written your first five chunks, revisioned your book as necessary, and selected your next chunks to write, you might want to sit down and make a writing schedule. I believe that such schedules are immensely useful. But if the very word "schedule" makes you cringe, you should know that a writing plan does not have to be detailed or onerous. A perfectly fine writing schedule might sound like any one of the following:

- "I'm going to write two hours every day except Sunday."
- "I'd like to create two chunks a week."
- "I'd like to write 20 pages this month."
- "I'd like to draft a thousand words each writing day."
- "Over the next two weeks I'd like to create a draft of chapter one."

Try to articulate your writing schedule for the next month.

YOUR OPENING CHUNK

The first few pages of your nonfiction book are your book's most important ones. In those pages you endeavor to interest a reader in your material and grab her attention. Therefore, you are likely to be concerned about getting that chunk written early and written well. But it is unlikely that you will arrive at the opening chunk of your book until you have thought about your book a lot, written many chunks, and revised and revisioned your book as necessary. Indeed, if you try to write your opening chunk before you have a good idea of what your book intends to be about and then stubbornly let that first opening stand, you are likely to do your book a significant disservice.

Remember that readers are only interested in a subject after the mind of the writer has worked on it. We don't want Einstein's earliest speculations, we want his theories of relativity. We don't want to know everything an expert on herbs has learned over a lifetime, we want information that we can use. The work a writer does when she synthesizes her raw information can happen in an instant or it can take 20 years, but still it must be accomplished. The writer has to figure out what her experiences meant, what she learned from them, and what information she wants to communicate to another person. For these reasons your opening chunk may be one of the last things you write.

Consider the following opening gambit for a book about a writer's experiences with her depression:

"Like many Americans, I have suffered from clinical depression. The DSM-IV (*Diagnostic and Statistical Manual of the American Psychiatric Association,* 4th ed., used by psychotherapists to diagnose mental illness) says about major depression that 'a person with depressed mood will usually describe feeling sad, hopeless, discouraged, down in the dumps, or some other colloquial equivalent.' This could have been written about me."

What the writer is actually saying in this opening gambit, to herself first of all but also to readers, is "I don't know yet what I want to talk about in this book, but it feels safe to begin by defining clinical depression. How can I go wrong with that?" But in fact she can go wrong—she already has gone wrong—because readers know, without necessarily knowing why, that the writer hasn't thought her subject through yet. She hasn't digested her material, made choices, or constructed meaning. This opening is generic—it is an unengaged, unprocessed place marker. From the point of view of grammar, style, or logic there is nothing wrong with it. But it has no meaning.

This opening might be fine for a college paper in an abnormal psychology class, where the goal is not to provide a unique look at clinical depression but rather an adequate summation of the known. The college writer does not have to go deep, reveal secrets, or stretch emotionally. Even if she added a few personal experiences, she could easily do so without providing any meaning; some celebrity tell-all books, for instance, are so guarded, contrived, and empty that we know that the writer's primary goal was to reveal nothing. The college writer, too, does not have to make meaning in order to write an adequate paper. All she has to do is cut and paste from her research sources and cut and paste from her personal anecdotes.

If one of my college students began her paper this way, I'd be pleased enough. It is logical, informative, and better than most openings I've seen, both in college papers and nonfiction books. But you will want to do more, because you want your book to be special, eloquent, and meaningful.

Consider these alternative opening gambits for a memoir on depression:

"The third time I was hospitalized for clinical depression, I fell in love with shock treatment."

"They say that the surest sign that your clinical depression has lifted is that you can smile again. I haven't smiled since I was nine—four decades ago."

"My first psychiatrist was Jewish. Each time I went back to my studio after therapy sessions I painted swastikas. I hated what he said about me—not what he said, but what I could read in his eyes—and I took my anger out on the Jews."

"It was while my husband was raping me in my hospital bed that I realized that I wanted a divorce."

These better openings couldn't come into existence until the writer had thought about her material and done some writing on her book. As she thought and wrote she began to understand what her book was really about, what tone she meant to take, which experiences felt like they would fit in the narrative and which wouldn't, what kind of organizational scheme she wanted to employ, and so on. At some point— maybe at the split second of inception, but maybe not for a week, a month, or many months later—she suddenly *knew* where her book would begin. That is a happy moment!

Be assured that you, too, will eventually arrive at the right opening for your book. Just continue writing chunks and acquiring a better sense of your book's intentions. A third goal, in addition to writing chunks and learning about your book, is to brainstorm the sections of your nonfiction book proposal. In chapters 6–11, I will offer strategies for creating a strong, effective nonfiction book proposal, beginning in chapter 6 with strategies for producing the credentials section of your proposal.

CREATING YOUR
CREDENTIALS SECTION

I f I were to ask you to tell me a little bit about yourself, your answer
would vary depending on whether I was your new physician, your
new financial planner, a director auditioning you for a play, or an
editor interested in purchasing and publishing your book. In the
first case you'd inform me about any allergic reactions to antibiotics
you'd had in the past, in the second case you'd tell me about your experiences with the stock market, and in the third case you'd share with
me your work history in the theater. But how would you answer if I
were an editor?

That would depend in part on the book you were writing. Say that
you have the expertise to write several different books: a narrative
memoir, a technical book about some aspect of your professional work,
and a history book about the subject you've been studying for decades
as a hobbyist. If you are writing a narrative memoir, I need to find your
story and your circumstances interesting and moving, which means
that I need a powerful voice from you rather than dry details. If you are

telling me about your professional book, I would like to hear that you have the right professional credentials, that you are an expert in your field, and that you regularly present the ideas in your book to other professionals. If you are showing me a proposal for a history book, I want to know about the extent of your studies, the originality of your research, and your membership in groups interested in your subject.

If I am trying to sell an editor a book on sleep thinking, I present my credentials one way, emphasizing my lifelong interest in sleep research and the existence of my sleep thinking newsletter. If I am trying to sell her a book on dancers' business survival skills, I present my credentials another way, emphasizing the fact that I have worked with dancers for two decades as a creativity coach. If I am trying to sell her a book on communication tips, I present my credentials a third way, leading with the fact that I am a licensed family therapist. In each case I am making meaning, just as I endeavor to make meaning when I write. But here the meaning I am making is autobiographical meaning. I am creating the right me.

You will make this autobiographical meaning in the credentials section of your book proposal, a section usually called "about the author." It is typically from one to three pages in length, is written in the third person, and contains many specifics about your history and your experiences. In addition, it lays out a certain amount of marketing information (business organizations you belong to, talks you have given on the subject of your book, etc.). In this section you endeavor to express yourself well, highlight your most appropriate credentials, and demonstrate to editors that you will be an asset in the marketing and promotion of your book.

How important is the credentials section of your book proposal? Extremely important. It isn't a pro forma part of the book proposal but a vital part, right up there with the quality of your idea, the quality of your writing, your demonstration of a need for your book, and the strength of your marketing and promotion plan. Expressing your credentials effectively and presenting the most relevant facts helps you, and penning a boring version of your autobiography and leaving out salient points hurts you. Indicating that you see yourself as exclusively an author lessens your chances of publication, and expressing a desire to market—especially as evidenced by past deeds—increases your chances. Your credentials section can do you a lot of good or a lot of harm.

Picture a typical editor. She has decided to read three nonfiction book proposals on her commute home, proposals that she's pulled from her large pile of recently received proposals and given a quick once-over at the office. Each of these three book proposals describes a reasonably interesting and somewhat marketable book. She decides to read the credentials section of each proposal to help her make up her mind.

1. The first proposal is for a book called *Mesquite Barbecue Cooking.* The author mentions that several of his poems have been published, that he has a degree in creative writing, and that he traveled with rock bands for eight years, during which time he collected barbecue recipes from performers on tour and from restaurants around the country.

2. The second proposal is for a book called *Long Year Out,* a memoir about the author's adventures living among the tribespeople of New Guinea. The credentials she highlights are her undergraduate degree in anthropology, the fact that she has traveled extensively, and her love of ethnographies.

3. The third proposal is for a book called *Cure Your Arthritis!* In the credentials section the author, a former arthritis sufferer now in her mid-sixties, explains that she has studied herbal healing practices with several Indian practitioners and cured her own arthritis using herbs.

The credentials these authors chose to highlight are unlikely to impress this editor very much. Indeed, she will be tempted to pass on all three book proposals, solely on the basis of her feeling that these authors' credentials are unlikely to impress people—like her publisher and her sales force—who need to stand behind a book she purchases. There is nothing wrong with these authors' credentials, but they are neither strong enough nor exciting enough to convince her to champion one of these books.

But what if the first author had said that the lead-off recipe in his proposal was Mick Jagger's favorite barbecue recipe and that the second recipe was for a dish that Elton John regularly served at barbecues for the Queen? That would make a profound difference. By not alerting this editor to the fact that famous rock stars had shared with him their favorite barbecue recipes, this author failed to present his credentials in their best light. With this new information our editor might see a *Rock Star Recipes* book in her mind's eye, which would probably interest her considerably more than a *Mesquite Barbecue Recipe* book.

What if the second author, rather than highlighting her academic and intellectual credentials, had explained that she had participated in 20 mind-altering kava rituals while in New Guinea and had been allowed to hunt and spear fish with the men? Many tens of thousands of people have degrees in anthropology and have read the standard ethnographies, but few have lived this kind of adventure. Her adventures are her best credentials, and by not mentioning them she badly hurt her chances of getting published.

What if the third author had said that, in addition to curing her own arthritis and studying with Indian practitioners, she also published an online arthritis newsletter that reached 10,000 readers every month? That significant piece of information scores many points for the author. First, it proves that a lot of people are interested in what she has to say. Second, it shows that she knows how to market herself. Third, it suggests that she can meet deadlines and handle feedback. Fourth, and most important, it moves her from "New Age kook with an herbal arthritis cure" to "expert with a constituency."

A WRITER WITH STRONG CREDENTIALS

The ideal credentials section conveys excellent credentials, clarity of expression, and the message that the author will be an asset in the life of her book. Let's take a look at one such ideal credentials section.

The following is a small portion of one author's credentials section. The client in question was a first-time author writing a book called *Lean and Green,* based on her experiences consulting with and interviewing corporate executives. Her goal in the book was to show business readers and the general public that corporations could be both profit-minded and environmentally aware.

About the Author

Pamela J. Gordon, Certified Management Consultant, is a leader and speaker in the worlds of business, professional associations, education, and the performing arts. She is president and founder of Technology Forecasters, Inc., a management consulting firm that for three years in a row has been named by the San Francisco Business Times as one of the 100 fastest-growing private companies in the Bay Area.

Ms. Gordon is a Certified Management Consultant, certified by the Institute of Management Consultants. She was President, and most recently Chair, of the Northern California Chapter, which is IMC's largest chapter. An avid speaker, Ms. Gordon commands several thousand dollars a day for speeches and consulting sessions and addresses audiences at high-tech firms and universities nationwide. Ms. Gordon has been quoted numerous times in more than 50 newspapers and magazines around the world, including *Fortune* and the *Wall Street Journal,* and has appeared on television and radio regarding high-tech business and manufacturing trends.

It won't surprise you to learn that the proposal for *Lean and Green* was chosen for representation by the first literary agent the author sent it to and that the agent managed to sell it quickly.

A credentials section of this sort is very persuasive. Why? Because of the author's *credentials.* She doesn't have to use language artfully to convince an editor that her background is impressive and that she knows how to market products. Her credentials speak for themselves. It is clear that she is an expert in her field and a proven marketer.

The best credentials section is the one written by the person with the best credentials. If you've had three bestsellers published, that puts you ahead of someone with no books published. If you invented the transplant machine you are writing about, that puts you ahead of physicians who merely use it. If you starred in a hit movie, that puts you ahead of the makeup artist on that movie. If you teach at Harvard, that puts you ahead of someone who teaches at a less known university. If you've given a hundred workshops in the past year on your subject, that puts you ahead of someone who has yet to create a workshop.

That isn't to say that a person with limited credentials can't get her book published. But it does mean that a person in that position will want to do two things: express the credentials she does have very well and beef up her credentials.

EFFECTIVELY EXPRESSING THE CREDENTIALS
YOU HAVE

Writers often harm themselves by not being explicit enough when the time comes to articulate their credentials. A writer will say that she has "worked with many large companies" when in fact she has been hired as a consultant by IBM, Cisco, Microsoft, and Apple and reported directly to the CEO of each of these companies. I had a client with exactly these credentials who expressed them so mildly that you would have thought that she did luncheon presentations for middle management. It put you to sleep imagining her credentials as she first expressed them, but it woke you up to think that CEOs of giant corporations were hanging on her every word.

I try to pay attention to being explicit and detailed whenever I express my credentials in a new book proposal. For example, I could say something bland like "I have done many radio interviews" when I talk about my media experience. That phrase would count for something. But it hardly resonates in the ear. Consider how much better the following sounds:

"In support of a recent book, *Twenty Communication Tips for Families,* I did thirty radio interviews during a two-week period. I joined Drew Mariani of the Catholic Family Network on a show that aired live in 10 major markets. I did Mike Haga's *On the Brink* show syndicated to 160 stations. I spoke with Annette Blanchard of KUCI in Los Angeles and Emily Elfenbein of WBEB, Philadelphia, one of that city's highest-rated stations. I spent a great hour with Frank Foster of WWBA, Tampa, and an excellent 45 minutes with Tom Pope on his show syndicated to 12 stations. During those two weeks I appeared on shows that aired in every major American market and 90 countries worldwide."

Even if your credentials are modest and you don't have that many explicit announcements to make, it is still your choice whether you will be lively or dull, energetic or lazy, smart or the opposite. In each of the following pairs, which sentence does a better job of expressing the writer's credentials? Is there any question in your mind?

1. "As the shaman of my village, I performed many duties."
2. "As the shaman of my village I was entrusted with finding water, curing disease, casting off spells, and insuring a bountiful harvest."

1. "I've lived a pretty interesting life and people will be moved by my story."
2. "When Stalin sent me to the Gulag, he thought he had pronounced my death sentence. But I fooled him by learning how to live on snow and rat droppings."

1. "Everybody loves my chili recipes and you will too."
2. "The only time I ever lost a chili cooking contest was the time Texas Bob stole my cumin. Making chili without cumin is like making love without touching. I didn't stand a chance."

In order to create the right me, I use language to my benefit. For instance, I call myself "internationally known." A handful of readers in various parts of the world have read my books. I've gotten e-mail from readers in New Zealand, Singapore, London, Vienna, Rome, and so on. Perhaps two hundred subscribers to my newsletters live in foreign countries. I am not "internationally known" the way Tiger Woods or Julia Roberts is internationally known, but my claim does not stretch the truth out of shape.

I say that I "founded and wrote *Callboard Magazine*'s 'Staying Sane in the Theater' column," which is precisely and literally true. But I do not add that *Callboard Magazine* is a service magazine for San Francisco Bay Area actors (didn't it sound like a Hollywood, New York, or national magazine to your ear?), that I wrote the column for only about a year, or that it was dropped. Why would I say those things? Why would you?

Whether you have limited credentials, modest credentials, or excellent credentials, you still have the task of presenting your credentials in a compelling fashion. Imagine that three different people want to write the survival guide for actors called *Elephant and Rat* that I described in the previous chapter. The following are brief examples of how these individuals might do a worse job or a better job of expressing their credentials.

1. First theater person, limited acting credentials, credentials expressed poorly:

Although I haven't done that much acting since high school, I have attended a few local acting classes and even auditioned for some roles in community theater. But I have a friend who has managed to carve out a life in repertory theater and her life really fascinated me, so I thought I would take a peek at what it takes to be a working actor, using a lot of her story as illustrative examples. She's also told me stories about other actors and those stories will give the book some added punch.

2. First theater person, limited acting credentials, credentials expressed well:

I am student of the theater and an actor. Although I made my life away from the theater, I have never stopped taking acting classes or participating in community theater. My admiration for the working actor has only grown, and I've made it my business to learn what sets apart actors who make a living from their art from those who end up abandoning the theater life. *Elephant and Rat* is my exploration of the survival skills of the working actor.

1. Second theater person, modest acting credentials, credentials expressed poorly:

I've done a bit of acting in community and local theater, as much as I could, considering that I am also a parent and part-time website designer. I always wished that I could make the theater my life, but I had to give that idea up, because I wouldn't make the move to New York or L.A. and because, as a mother, I needed a steadier income than the theater affords. But I remained pretty curious about the life of the actor, kept jotting down notes as ideas came to me, and finally got down to putting those notes together. I think the results are pretty interesting.

2. Second theater person, modest acting credentials, credentials expressed well:

All my life I've had a love affair with the theater. I fashioned a career in the computer industry, but I never stopped acting, and I've had a highly successful part-time acting career for the past dozen years, including important roles in several contemporary dramas and revivals. The lives of working actors fascinated me, and during the run of each play I would ask my fellow cast members what skills helped them maintain their spirits and their acting careers. These conversations and my further research led me to understand exactly what survival skills every working actor needs to master.

1. Third theater person, excellent acting credentials, credentials expressed poorly:

I've loved theater all my life and I know a few things about that odd, often maligned creature, the actor. Who hasn't wondered what makes an actor tick? How do any actors manage to survive? I've seen actors shoot themselves in the foot, ruin relationships, even appear on stage drunk. What separates the actor who gets work from the rest of the membership of SAG and AFTRA? Exactly the things I'm going to talk about in my book.

2. Third theater person, excellent acting credentials, credentials expressed well:

In my 20 years in the theater I've acted in 23 major productions, hundreds of smaller productions, and directed 7 others. I've also appeared in 12 films, done scores of industrials, and appeared in over 50 commercials. My production of Bertolt Brecht's *Mother Courage* won the June Singer award as the finest repertory theater production of the year, and I have been nominated for three Tony Awards and one Oscar. As an acting teacher I've helped nearly a thousand actors, many of them world-famous ones, master the craft of acting *and* the art of surviving as an actor. I know firsthand what skills it takes for an actor to make a career in regional theater.

Exercise : YOUR SPECIFIC CREDENTIALS WITH RESPECT TO THE BOOK YOU ARE WRITING

The goal of an author preparing her credentials section for an ocean rowing book is to brainstorm a list of **everything** in her life, no matter how small or obscure, that directly pertains to ocean rowing and her ocean rowing expertise, including the significant facts that she is a world-class ocean rower and the author of many articles on ocean rowing but also including the facts that her grandfather first introduced her to rowing when she was six and that she has river-rowed on the Thames, the Danube, the Liffey, and eight other major European rivers.

That is your goal, too, to brainstorm a complete list of your credentials specific to this book. Instead of saying that you've written articles, name those articles. Instead of saying that you've gathered macaroni and cheese recipes from around the world, list the various trips you took (to Madison, to Milan, etc.) that informed your understanding of how macaroni and cheese could be prepared. Be explicit and comprehensive and produce several pages of relevant information.

Exercise : YOUR GENERAL CREDENTIALS FOR BEING TAKEN SERIOUSLY

Anything in your life that makes you look accomplished, professional, connected, marketable, interesting, special, good at public speaking, or good at selling might ultimately be useful to include in your credentials sections. Think about any time that you:

- Spoke in public
- Managed a project to completion
- Received praise
- Got certified or licensed
- Were interviewed
- Were singled out for recognition
- Marketed something
- Were written about
- Attended a special class
- Got a degree
- Promoted something
- Impressed someone
- Associated with celebrities
- Had an unusual or unique experience

Generate a comprehensive list of experiences of this sort, including anything that might put you in a good light, impress another person, or make you look interesting or unique.

BEEFING UP YOUR CREDENTIALS

Very often I have to beef up my credentials in order to create the right me on paper and in order to be the right me to write a given book.

I may have to do research that I hadn't intended to do, go out and have new experiences, try my idea out in a workshop and get feedback on it, or solicit help from people who know the territory I'm writing about. For instance, I recently led a six-week teleclass—a phone class where students are connected to one another and to me via a phone bridge—because I want to be able to say that I lead teleclasses. I can't say that I lead teleclasses unless I have given at least one. But having given just that one, I can and will say that "I lead teleclasses." I beef up my credentials in reality, then I use language to make that new credential sound as good as it can sound.

The act of leading one workshop makes you a workshop leader. The fact that you publish a quarterly column in your local writers' club newsletter makes you a newsletter columnist. The moment you are interviewed about anything you become "familiar with the interview process." That is how language works and is meant to work. You *are* a workshop leader, newsletter columnist, and familiar with the interview process in these scenarios. A book proposal is not an academic paper but a sales tool in which you sell your idea and yourself. Become a new, improved you by acquiring some new credentials, then stand behind them by the strong language you use.

Agents and editors will think more highly of your project if you are an expert in your field, if you've already published on your subject, if you've led workshops and seminars, if you have connections with writers and producers in television, radio, and the print media, and so on. Therefore, it will be an extremely good idea for you to work on boosting your credentials by writing articles, giving workshops in your community, becoming an online expert—by, in short, doing everything in your power to make yourself appear more professional, accomplished, marketable, and attractive.

What specifically can you do? Any (or several, or all) of the following:

1. Present your material in public. Give a talk at your local library or to your religious group. Give your talk several times in front of different audiences.

2. Start a newsletter. Create an online newsletter that you send out monthly, first to a few friends and then to more and more people as you promote your newsletter through online affinity groups, your public presentations, and so on.

3. Submit articles or essays for publication. Take your best chunk and turn it into a stand-alone article or essay.

4. Contact experts in your field and enter into conversation and correspondence with them.

5. Prepare and lead workshops. The "Extracting Principles" exercise on page 75 can help you organize a workshop on your subject that, to begin with, you can offer for free to religious, civic, business, or professional groups.

6. Prepare and teach classes. Most colleges and universities offer extended education classes taught by experts outside the faculty and most cities and towns have a civic arts or leisure arts organization that sponsors classes for members of the community. Prepare a one-day class, a weekend class, or a class that runs for several weeks, determine which local venues would be most appropriate for your class, and contact them with your class idea.

7. Join relevant organizations and become active in them. If your memoir focuses on issues like alcoholism, spousal abuse, or incest, become involved in relevant support organizations that will want to announce your memoir when it is published.

8. Speak publicly about subjects not related to your book. You can give a speech or two at Toastmasters, join a "talking circle" group to practice your presentation skills, or volunteer to host the awards night at your business. It is good experience—and a credit in your credentials section—to have made any kind of public presentation.

What is the "perfect" author package? A charismatic celebrity expert. A beautiful woman who also happens to be America's best-known psychic, relationship counselor, or pop investment guru. A media-savvy fellow who does two hundred workshops a year and knows the home numbers of television producers. These and people like them are the people with whom you are competing. You are competing with people who have 20,000 subscribers to their newsletters, whose websites get thousands of hits a day, whose names are known to producers as the pundit to call if a guest cancels or if a news story breaks. If you were an editor, would you want that person's next book or yours?

Your only way to compete, if you are not this celebrity guru, is to do the best work you can in all facets of your job: to have a strong idea that is well articulated, to present a reasonable but nevertheless compelling marketing and promotion plan, to do a fine job of explaining why your book will be wanted, and so on. You want to think well, write well, sell well, and look good on paper. Anything that helps you look good on paper is worth doing, whether that's publishing an article, giving a talk, leading a group, or being interviewed in a magazine.

Exercise : BUILDING YOUR CREDENTIALS

Make a plan to boost your credentials in the next weeks and months, while you are building your book and your book proposal. If you are writing a cookbook, can you enter one of your dishes in a cooking competition (and, one hopes, win!)? If you are writing a guide to on-line banking services, can you give an online class in the subject and begin to call yourself a teacher and workshop leader? If you are writing a memoir, can you craft some articles out of your budding book and submit them to appropriate magazines? Think about what you can do to make yourself look like—and actually become—more of an expert on your chosen topic.

Try to list 50 or 100 things you might do. Then sit with your list and choose the best two or three to do right away and the best two or three long-term possibilities. Do those first two or three things in the next few days. Set up a plan and a schedule for tackling your long-term objectives and commit to following them.

Exercise : **CREATING YOUR CREDENTIALS SECTION**

Using the material that you generated from the exercises in this chapter, and taking into account credentials that you plan to obtain but do not have yet, write a draft of your credentials section. Revise it as many times as necessary until it is as complete and compelling as you can make it.

After you've created your credentials section, it is a good idea to keep updating it as your credits and accomplishments mount. An editor needs to feel confident about you on many levels if she is going to purchase your book: confident that you are expert enough to write your book, confident that you will energetically support your book, confident that you can handle interviews and book signings and talk sensibly about your subject. The credentials section is the place where you convince her that you are up to these demands.

CREATING YOUR COMPETING AND COMPLEMENTARY BOOKS SECTION

I n a book proposal you are trying to sell a number of things. You are trying to sell your book idea. You are trying to sell yourself as a writer, an authority, and a salesperson. You are trying to sell the fact that markets exist for your book. And you are trying to sell an agent or editor on the idea that your book will be a welcome addition to the literature on your subject. Agents and publishers need to be able to place your book in the context of already existing books if they are to feel confident that your book can survive—and hopefully thrive—among related books already on the market.

Let's say that you've decided to write a book about barbecuing on heated lava rocks. If your book is the twelfth book on this subject, why would someone buy yours? Have the other 11 been out of print for a decade? That would be important information to include in your proposal. Are you offering something special, like the fact that those authors garnered their recipes from secondary sources while yours are from the master Hawaiian chef who invented this barbecuing technique? If another book is already a bestseller in this area, does that mean that there is a nice market for books of this sort or does it mean that the market is sewn up by that major title? If I am an editor who is interested in your proposal, these are things that I need to know.

Questions of this sort are answered in the competing and complementary books section of your book proposal. The central question that this section answers is *What distinguishes my book from other books on the market?* The answer to this may be that you have special expertise or many unique experiences, your organizational frame or guiding metaphor is strong and original, other books on your subject have failed to take certain facts into account, some of the books on the market are outdated, others are more academic and narrow than yours, and so on.

The purpose of the competing and complementary books section of your book proposal is not to suggest that your book will be bought by "everybody who loves a good book." You aren't out to imply that, because it is warm and appealing, your book will do as well as the *Chicken Soup* books; because it is light and amusing, it will do as well as *A Year in Provence;* because it is poignant and memorable, it will do as well as *Angela's Ashes.* This "hopeful associating" doesn't impress publishers much. Nor will it pay you to produce a list of four hundred books vaguely related to yours, three hundred of which are out of print and only two of which are actually on point.

Your job is to help an editor understand why there is a need for your book and why your book will float to the top of a sea already awash with books. First, this means understanding what your book is about. Second, it means researching the marketplace. Third, it means crafting distinctions between your book and books like it. Fourth, it means associating your book in meaningful (and not merely hopeful) ways with books that readers have actually purchased. Last, this means using your rhetorical skills to convince a skeptical editor that she should steward your book through editorial meetings.

For each book that you select for inclusion in this section, you identify it (by title, author, publisher, date of publication, and price), describe it in a few sentences, and distinguish your book from it in some way that places your book in its best light. Some factors you should take into account as you think about selecting books for inclusion in your competing and complementary books section are the following.

1. This section of your book proposal helps an editor locate your book geographically. Where can it be shelved in a bookstore, since many books can be logically shelved in more than one section? A self-help book might sensibly belong not only in a bookstore's self-help section but also in the business section, if it explains the psychological obstacles to effective leadership. A cookbook might be shelved both in the cookbook section and the travel section, if it has breezy place descriptions along with its recipes.

We all think that our books are one-of-a-kind, so it can be difficult to imagine jamming your special project on a shelf with what seem to you vastly different titles. But the fact is, if your book is published it will need to be shelved in an already-existing category in a bookstore. So it would benefit you to make yourself familiar with bookstore categories. Go to a bookstore—or to several—and look around.

It may very well be that there is no category that exactly suits your book. You need to then identify the next closest category. Simply saying that your book goes in the New and Noteworthy Nonfiction section isn't an option. Only a very few brand-new books out of all those books published end up in that section and publishers are most interested in knowing where your book will be located after it's been out for a few months, when it becomes what is called "backlist." Looking around a bookstore is therefore a very important part of your job as a nonfiction writer.

2. You will want to have some idea of what categories and territories already exist and you will want to think about which categories and territories are growing and which are shrinking. In 1990, there was no such thing as a special shelving category for Internet books. Today it is a thriving subsection of the business category. On the other hand, it would be hard today to sell an agent or publisher on an "inner child" or "codependency" book, because these once popular ideas sound passé now. Information on growing and shrinking bookstore sections will help you for two reasons: you will be able to talk to agents and editors intelligently in your book proposal about where your book might be located, and you will be able to talk to yourself intelligently about whether you want to move your book this way or that so that it fits in a stronger category in the marketplace.

3. You will also want to place your book in its chronological context. What similar books have come out before yours and what, if any, books are coming out in the future? Note that publishers are mostly concerned with recent books in your line. If you were writing a book about some aspect of Jungian thought, for example, in your comparison section you would focus on similar recent books and perhaps explain how Jung's ideas have been recently popularized in related books about character type and personality style. But it would be of little interest to an editor to know what and when Jung himself published or what important books in the 1940s, 1950s, and 1960s made use of Jung's ideas.

4. In this section you will also want to locate your book idea in the context of other ideas. If you are writing a cookbook about using garlic, then it is a cookbook. But if you are writing a cookbook about garlic that plays with the idea that garlic is an aphrodisiac and you call it *Garlic for Lovers,* then you might want an editor or agent to picture your book shelved in the cookbook section but promoted and marketed with books on romance and relationships for Valentine's Day.

5. You also want to consider how narrowly or broadly to focus your comparison section. In placing your *Garlic for Lovers* book in context, you could compare it exclusively to other garlic-for-lovers books (a narrow approach), to other romantic cookbooks or other garlic cookbooks (a middle approach), or to all cookbooks (a broad approach). A good plan is to make sure you cover the books most like yours in sufficient detail that an agent or editor understands how yours differs (and is better). Then you can touch on the broader context to help her place your book in her mind and whet her appetite for its category.

6. The competing and complementary books section is also the place to put in context whatever makes your book special or unusual. If you see it as integral to your book's meaning that it has color illustrations throughout, then you need to include examples of other books like yours that have been successful in part because they included beautiful illustrations. If it is essential that your book have a small or unique trim size, you need to point out other books, similar in theme to yours, that have been successful in part because of their appealing size.

Taking all of these factors into consideration can feel like a daunting challenge. For this reason would-be nonfiction writers often balk at creating this section of their book proposal, either putting off this task until the last minute and making a hash of it or taking the shortcut of comparing their book to only one or two others. But it isn't only because they have so much to consider that they avoid this work. They are also inclined to avoid examining existing books because books that are similar to theirs have the power to cause them to change the focus of their book and even to abandon their project altogether.

EXISTING LITERATURE AS THREAT AND AGENT OF CHANGE

If you happened to read books in your field before you began conceiving and writing your book, you wouldn't have experienced those books as threatening. Now that you have a book idea and a book to write, however, the situation has changed. Say, for example, that you are writing a book on business survival skills for actors and are informed in a book you're reading, written by a theater producer with impeccable credentials, that actors can't live on repertory theater income alone. Not only did you think that they could, but you based your book idea on that thesis. Because this author's opinion, if factually correct, undermines your thesis, you must take this troubling new information into account.

Maybe the author has lumped together nonpaying and low-paying community theater with better-paying professional repertory theater, and a careful reading of his book will bring that happy news to light. If the author is indeed talking about repertory theater only, maybe the facts of the matter have changed since his book was written and some research will reveal that the situation has changed. If, however, the author turns out to be right, you will have to embrace what he says and change your book's emphasis, focusing on the need for actors to cobble together income from several sources, even if they are employed full-time in a repertory company.

Encountering books in your subject area is bound to have an impact on your own book idea and what you had intended to say. A lot of what you read will not cause you to change your approach or focus, but some of it will. If you research your book's competition before committing to its organizational frame or its central idea, this threat is minimized. But even then, you are likely to find yourself on a roller-coaster ride as the differing opinions of the authors you read force you to continually alter your ideas. For this reason, even in cases where they have no choice in the matter, as for instance if they are preparing a dissertation that requires them to have a comprehensive knowledge of their subject, would-be authors regularly feel too threatened to dive in.

Can we skip doing this reading and exploring? Not entirely. But we may be able to keep it to a minimum, to skim rather than read, and to quickly dismiss a lot of what we encounter. If we have given our book idea the thought it deserves, we are likely to feel secure about the integrity of our central idea. We may be sure, for instance, that it is hard for actors to earn a living, not easy, and therefore we can dismiss writers who put on a happy face and claim that every would-be actor can become a star. We may be sure that the business survival skills we've identified are in fact crucial and can dismiss writers who claim that actors should remain emotionally vulnerable at all times (when we know that a thick skin is also required) or who argue that actors are by nature sociable (when we know that they tend to be more introverted than extroverted). The more sure we are of our own ideas, the easier it is for us to make our way safely through the competing literature.

Exercise : **AFFIRMING SELF-WORTH AND FLEXIBILITY**

As you encounter books in your subject area, you want to retain the sense that you will ultimately present good ideas in your book. But you must also accept that your current ideas may change as you read what others have written. You have two things to affirm: your self-worth and your willingness to remain flexible.

As an exercise, create an affirmation (a sentence that supports an intention) that expresses these two ideas. An example might be "My book may change as I read in the existing literature, but my ideas are good and ultimately I will arrive at the right destination." Once you've created your affirmation, practice saying it until you firmly believe it.

The thought of confronting the existing literature is daunting in another sense as well. We often don't know how to think about the phrase "books like mine," especially considering that our book is not written and may be changing shape from day to day. When I list books similar to mine, do I mean physically similar, as in trim size or length, or do I mean similar in content or approach? The answer depends on what I've chosen as the key element of my book. If my book is an un-usual length or trim size, then comparing it to others on the basis of its physical attributes is not irrelevant. If I am writing a travel book, do I intend to compare it with other travel books on the basis of the geographical area that is covered or on the basis of a specific focus, such as traveling cheaply, traveling with pets, or traveling with kids? Is my goal to find the one book that is most like mine or to find scores of books that have some feature or features in common with mine?

Your goal in comparing your book to the competition is to present your book in its best light without falsifying the facts. If books in your subject area have come out in a regular stream for many years, you might use this to your advantage by laying out the competition chronologically, with your book at the pinnacle. If you are writing in a narrow niche, as a colleague of mine who explains the principles of acting to animators does, the approach that puts your book in its best light is one that emphasizes the limited competition and the very "niche-ness" of your title, with its small but dedicated audience.

Whatever approach you decide to take in your comparison section should be logical and self-serving—as well as honest. If you discover that a recent book from a major publisher is very similar to your intended book, it isn't a good idea to act as if that book doesn't exist, even though a publisher or agent may never discover your omission. Rather, you want to explain how your book is different from its rival. In this way a negative becomes a positive. The book you happened on complements your book as well as competes with it and serves as proof that a market exists for your idea. Therefore, you do not need to feel too disappointed when you discover that books similar to yours are already on the market or wonder if you should hide their existence from editors.

In addition to feeling somewhat threatened by existing books and unsure of how to think about the phrase "books like mine," you will probably feel woefully ignorant. Unless you began your project by thoroughly researching other books in your field, you are probably not very aware of the range of publications that are out there. Why should you be? Even if you are a professional with a need to keep up on your subject matter, it's unlikely that you would keep tabs on every new book in your field. You would probably only be aware of a few books that have been reviewed or discussed in your professional magazines and not have read more than one or two of those. Virtually no one will have read every new book in her field or have even a cursory awareness of the breadth and depth of books in her subject area.

Therefore, your starting point is likely one of ignorance. This is natural and should not frighten you away from your project. You can expect to feel a little ignorant as you confront the existing literature and even more ignorant as you learn about the books that exist. But you can help yourself feel less anxious about all this "not knowing" if you just remind yourself that it is natural and inevitable and that your core idea is unlikely to be shaken by what you encounter in other books. The work you have done up to this point has already convinced you that the creation of your nonfiction book is a process requiring your thought, attention, and courage. Now you can bring the same qualities to an examination of the existing literature.

DISTINGUISHING YOUR BOOK
FROM SIMILAR BOOKS

As you encounter books that are similar to yours, you will want to articulate how your project is different from and in some sense better than each of them. If you have 10 similar books to discuss in your comparison section, you may find yourself using 10 different comparisons. One book that, like yours, is rich in detail may be usefully out of date. Another book may be up-to-the-minute but short on ideas. A third book may have treated your subject in a reader-unfriendly, academic way while a fourth book may have popularized your subject to the point of oversimplicity. The distinction that you want to make with respect to each of these books is different case-by-case.

There are countless ways that you can distinguish your book from the competition. Here are 20 possibilities.

1. Is your book based based on more up-to-date research?
2. Does it fill a niche left by other books?

3. Does it provide its information in a more accessible format than other books?

4. Is it based on unique or more interesting personal experiences?

5. Does your book take your subject to the next logical step?

6. Does your book target audiences and markets not reached by other books?

7. Does it present a new idea?

8. Does it synthesize ideas into a new theory or a new whole?

9. Does it look at material that hasn't been explored for some time?

10. Does your book take a subject that has only been treated in an academic way and popularize it?

11. Have you included material known only to you, gathered via interviews, research, life experience, and so on?

12. Do you make clear ideas that other authors have not been able to clarify?

13. Have you taken a new, controversial position on a well-known subject?

14. Does your writing capture the flavor of an era, a locale, a movement, and so on, in ways that previous books haven't?

15. Have you been given access to material unavailable to previous authors?

16. Is your book better researched than previous books on the subject?

17. Is your book organized around a powerful metaphor that brings new life to the subject?

18. Does it have a special appeal because of the voice you bring to the material?

19. Is your book shorter and easier to digest than other books on the subject?

20. Is it more comprehensive than other books on the subject?

CHRONOLOGICAL, THEMATIC, AND LIST APPROACHES

You are likely to come upon scores of books that are in some sense similar to yours. With each, you have two decisions to make: whether it contains anything that will be useful to you in writing your book and whether it belongs in your book comparison section. A book from a hundred years ago may provide you with good ideas but its antiquity makes it an unlikely candidate for your section. Conversely, a book may bore you or strike you as silly but has to be included in your comparison section because it is the best-known book in your field or because it is the book closest in subject matter to yours.

GOOD CHOICES FOR YOUR COMPARISON SECTION

The following are four good reasons to include a given book in your comparison section.

1. **The book is widely read by people interested in your subject.** An agent or publisher may not know that a certain title is the most popular book on your subject, but as an expert in your field you would. By comparing your book to the most popular book similar to yours, you plant the seed that your book may become quite popular also.
2. **The book is very recent.** Recent books demonstrate in what direction your subject is moving and point to any "new and improved" thinking in your field. Information about recent books gives agents and publishers a picture of what appears to be of current interest to other publishers.
3. **The book is published by a major publisher.** While titles from small presses can and do perform well, editors and publishers are

more likely to consider your subject area viable if books on it have appeared from major publishers.

4. **The book has sold well.** It is unlikely that you can get actual sales figures on rival books, but you may be able to ascertain whether it's been on the **New York Times** bestseller list or some other major bestseller list, whether it's been widely reviewed, whether it's going to become a movie, and so on. Being able to point to bestsellers (or even strong sellers) in your subject area is a significant plus.

Once you decide which books ought to be included in your comparison section, you will want to look those titles over and decide about an organizational approach. There are three main approaches you can use: a chronological approach, a thematic approach, or a list approach.

In a *chronological approach* you go back a certain number of years and compare and contrast your book to the relevant books that have come out during that time. Books that have appeared in the last few years are the most important to mention, so restricting your time frame to the last five years or so is a good idea, unless that forces you to leave out important, still relevant books that appeared somewhat earlier.

The following is a competing and complementary books section organized in chronological fashion that a client of mine completed. It is from a book proposal for a book called *All Grown Up,* about parents in their fifties, sixties, and seventies effectively parenting their grown children.

Several books on the parenting of adult children have appeared in the 1980s and 1990s. The 1980s saw the publication of *The Not-So-Empty Nest* by Feuerstein and Roberts (1981), *Family Connec-*

tions: Parenting and Your Grown Children, by Maslow and Duggan (1982), *The Postponed Generation* (Littwin, 1986), *Boomerang Kids* (Okimoto and Stegall, 1987), and *Adult Children Who Won't Grow Up* (Graves and Stockman, 1988).

The 1990s saw the publication of *Making Peace with Your Adult Children* (Smith, 1991), a book that emphasizes the healing of severe rifts between the two generations. This was followed by *Grown Up Children, Grown Up Parents* (Lieber, 1994) and *Becoming a Wise Parent for Your Grown Child* (Frain and Clegg, 1997). While these two books are thoughtful, wide-ranging "how-to" books, they fail to address (as my book will) cultural changes in the latter half of the twentieth century that deeply affect how we approach parenting and how we view self-development, issues of parental aging, loneliness, and increased longevity, and the common phenomenon of vital parents in their seventies, eighties, and nineties parenting "children" who are themselves on the verge of becoming seniors or already seniors.

In addition to the books just listed, there have been a few books published on more limited topics under the general rubric of parents and adult children. These include *Friends for Life: Enriching the Bond Between Mothers and Their Adult Daughters* (Jonas and Nissenson, 1997), *When Sons and Daughters Choose Alternative Lifestyles* (Caplan, 1996), *My Turn: Women's Search for Self After the Children Leave* (Shapiro, 1996), and *The Nesting Syndrome: Grown Children Living at Home* (Winer, 1997).

A second approach you might take is a *thematic approach,* in which you demonstrate how your book connects to similar books according to the ideas they contain. For example, your book on business survival skills for actors is thematically related to books on business survival skills for writers and business survival skills for visual artists, since creative and performing artists in the various disciplines face similar challenges. It would therefore be relevant to compare your book to a recent, good-selling book of this sort that was published by a major house. Your book is also thematically related to other books that contain interviews with actors, so you might compare your book to one or two well-received actors' interview books. Your book is also related to books that focus on actors who work in regional, community, and repertory theater, so comparing your book to important titles in this category also makes sense. In this way you produce a comparison section that is organized thematically, in which you compare your title with relevant titles in a number of categories.

The following thematic comparison section is from my proposal for a book called *The Van Gogh Blues: The Creative Person's Path Through Depression* (see the appendix for the complete proposal).

Only a handful of books have looked at the relationship between creativity and depression. All of these fall into two camps, those that presume that depression is biological and those that presume that it is psychological. The best-known book is one from the first camp, Kay Jamison's *Touched with Fire: Manic-Depressive Illness and the Artistic Temperament* (Free Press, 1993, paper), in which she argues that a wide variety of creative figures have had the "hereditary disease" of bipolar disorder (manic-depression). Her only advice for the creative person is to take antidepressants, and she offers no rationale for the connection between creativity and depression.

A similar book is Jablow Hershman's *Manic Depression and Creativity* (Prometheus Books, 1998, paper), which also offers no advice for the creative person suffering from depression.

Many books have been written that examine some aspect of creativity and depression from a psychological point of view or that look at a single creator's depression through the lens of psychology. These include Albert Lubin's *Stranger on the Earth: A Psychological Biography of Vincent van Gogh* (Holt, 1972, paper), Alice Miller's *The Untouched Key: Tracing Childhood Trauma in Creativity and Destructiveness* (Doubleday, 1990, paper), and John Gedo's *Portraits of the Artist* (Analytic Press, 1989, paper). These books, most of which argue from discredited psychoanalytic theory, have nothing to offer a creative person looking for help or hoping to understand her own depression.

There have also been a few first-person accounts, most notably William Styron's *Darkness Visible: A Memoir of Madness* (Random House, 1990) and Kay Jamison's bestselling memoir of her own manic-depressive illness. But no book has appeared that sets out to explain the relationship between creativity and depression and that sets as its goal *helping* creative people deal with depression. So far, all books in this genre have been descriptive and have been limited even in that regard by their reliance on unsupported biological and psychological theory. *The Van Gogh Blues* leaps ahead by presenting a new picture of creators' depression and by offering prescriptions, not descriptions.

It may turn out that neither a chronological approach nor a thematic approach works very well in your case. This happens often, as the books in a given subject area may be quite disparate and hard to connect to your book in a neat, logical way. Rather than straining to follow a time line when a time line makes no particular sense or endeavoring to produce categories when categories don't exist, you simply create a list of the books you want to discuss and distinguish your book from each comparison title in turn.

The author of *Lean and Green* found many books to include in her comparison section, but the titles she found did not lend themselves to a chronological or thematic approach. So she simply listed the fifteen titles she wanted to cover. The following are three entries from that list.

- *Green Marketing & Management: A Global Perspective,* by John F. Wasik, Blackwell, 1996, 247 pages, paperback, $27. Gives examples of goals that companies can set so as to profit from a commitment to environmental concerns. Focuses on marketing departments and managers, while *Lean and Green* appeals to every level of business and to consumers as well.

- *The Consumer's Guide to Effective Environmental Choices: Practical Advice from the Union of Concerned Scientists,* by Michael Brower, Ph.D., and Warren Leon, Ph.D., Crown (Three Rivers Press), 1999, 281 pages, paperback, $15. Gives practical advice to consumers about saving the planet. A book for consumers, it provides no guidance for individuals who want to change their company policies or bring lean and green ideas to the workplace.

- *Green, Inc.: A Guide to Business and the Environment,* by Frances Cairncross, Island Press, 1995, 277 pages, hardcover, $27. Analyzes the complex relationship among government, business, and the environment but fails to present hard evidence of companies profiting from environmental steps and therefore of limited appeal to business people.

To prepare a strong comparison section, take the following steps.

1. Research your subject by visiting bookstores, both virtual and real, libraries, and your own bookshelves. Focus on books widely read in your field, recent books, bestsellers, and titles published by major houses.

2. Gather identifying particulars on the books you deem relevant: title, author, publisher, date of publication, edition (hardback, trade paperback, or mass market paperback) and price. Use a separate sheet of paper to record the information about each of these titles.

3. For each book, note one or two ways that your book is different (and better) and describe those differences in a sentence or two.

4. Decide how you will organize your comparison section. Is a chronological, thematic, or list approach the most logical and compelling? Might a hybrid approach be necessary?

5. Create as many drafts of your comparison section as necessary. Do not consider yourself finished until you've produced a compelling section that does an excellent job of distinguishing your book from others on the market and articulating its rationale for existence.

You may find yourself puzzled about whether to include or exclude a certain book or category of books from your comparison section. You may feel that too many books like yours already exist or that, because no book like yours exists, yours must be a bad idea. You may grow anxious and begin to doubt your project. Be ready for these natural occurrences and expect your commitment to your project to be tested. If you manage to stay the course, you will have successfully produced one of the most important sections of your book proposal.

CREATING YOUR MARKETING
AND PROMOTION SECTION

The marketing and promotion section of your book proposal serves two distinct and vital functions. First, it helps agents and publishers visualize potential markets for your book. Second, it informs agents and publishers about the marketing and promotion efforts that you mean to undertake in support of your book. If you can convince these marketplace players that significant markets exist for your book and that your efforts will substantially increase its sales, you will have gone a long way toward securing interest in your book.

BEGINNER'S MIND

Each book you write, even if it is in the same general subject area as other books you've written, has its own market demographics and its own special appeal. For that reason you want to come to the task of identifying and articulating your book's various markets with what is called in Zen Buddhism "empty mind" or "beginner's mind." You may have supposed all along that you were writing your book for a certain group of people—serious actors, people who might be interested in ocean rowing, and so on—and imagine that now, as you approach your marketing and promotion section, that you can identify them in a sentence or two and be done with the matter. But if you were to do that, you would probably shortchange your book. The better process is to clear your mind and start fresh in thinking about your book's markets.

For example, I recently needed to identify the market for a book I'm writing on Internet creativity coaching, based on my experiences as a creativity coach and my work training new creativity coaches. My first thoughts were, "This a book for creativity coaches," and even more narrowly, "This is a book for people who take my trainings." But these are both very limited markets for this book. Rather than settle for a too-quick appraisal of my book's potential markets, I knew I had to step back and consider the matter of my book's markets.

The first thing I did was remind myself that I shouldn't expect to come up with all the answers instantly. Rather, it was more likely that some markets would come to me quickly and that additional markets would pop into my head over a period of hours, days, or weeks. As with every other aspect of creating a nonfiction book, I accepted the fact that identifying markets for my book was a process and not an event. I couldn't be done with it simply by brainstorming a list of markets and then finding good rhetorical devices to describe those markets.

My first efforts produced the following list:

- Creativity coaches (a small market, in the low thousands)
- People who take my trainings (on the order of hundreds)

- Potential clients of creativity coaches (a very large market composed of all creative and performing artists, on the order of one to two million self-identified artists, according to American Council for the Arts statistics)
- Psychotherapists and other helping professionals who want to learn how to counsel artists and effectively work with creativity issues like creative blockage, artistic anxiety, and so on.

Two days later I returned to the task of identifying additional markets for my Internet creativity coaching book. This time I had the following thoughts:

"A lot of hype has attached to the Internet, especially about its money-making potential for individuals who want to start a small business from home. I am actually making money training creativity coaches over the Internet, which would probably be of interest to a lot of folks who would like to see what a successful Internet consulting business looks like. So that is an additional market: people who are interested in Internet business possibilities."

This is the beginning process. I'm far from done at this point, because, even if I've identified all of my markets, I still have to help agents and editors visualize how these markets can be reached by providing specific information. But although I'm not done yet, you can see that there is nothing terribly mysterious or taxing about identifying markets for your book. This work is not so arduous or tricky that you couldn't do it over the course of a few days without too much sweat.

THE COURAGE TO LOOK AT YOUR BOOK'S MARKETS

Who are the likely purchasers of your book? At first glance you would think that an author would want to know the answer to this question. But arriving at an answer involves risking the possibility that you will begin to doubt your book's chances in the marketplace. You may be forced to recognize that there are only a small number of people who are likely to be interested in your subject matter, you may suddenly realize that were you to frame your book differently you might reach a much larger audience, and so on. Thinking about your book's markets may have a real impact on your book idea, and for this reason authors are often reluctant to focus on this important area.

Even though it may feel dangerous to think about your book's markets, you should embrace this work. It is better to understand the reality of your markets at this point in the process and to make decisions now about how you want to angle your material than to wait until you've written your book. Articulating potential markets for your book and evaluating whether you want to change the focus of your book will lead to a more marketable book and a stronger book proposal.

Exercise : **ANALYZE YOUR POTENTIAL MARKETS**

The first step in the process of determining your book's markets is to step back and attempt some objectivity. Begin by answering the following questions:

- For whom did I write this book? Who is its quintessential reader? If I wrote it for me, who am I and who are people like me?
- In addition to this quintessential reader, who else might be interested in this subject?
- Am I talking about a small segment of the population (say, people with three-car garages) or a large segment of the population (say, people who diet)? Can I put a number on this group? Can I find

some statistics about how many people own houses with three-car garages or have been on a diet in the last year?

- Are there a large number of readers who might be interested in my subject matter if I altered its focus, added additional material, or in some other way accommodated their needs?

- How can these potential readers best be reached? Are there certain publications that they read, for example trade journals or organization newsletters? Certain radio shows that they listen to? Certain television shows that they watch? Do they belong to certain organizations and/or attend certain conferences?

- If I began with several possible versions of my book idea, would one version reach a significantly larger audience than the others? Should I take that information into account in choosing which version of my book to write?

- Although my book is about one central thing (say, ocean rowing as a lifetime sport), is it also about other things each of which would interest an additional market (say, about weight maintenance or adventurous vacations)?

- When I sit with my table of contents and think about what I intend to include in each chapter, can I picture my material being of interest to additional people?

If the work you just did picturing potential markets for your book caused you to rethink your book's focus, you have probably made yourself feel a little ill. Possibly the chunks you've written no longer will work for this re-visioned version of your book; probably the competing and complementary books section is no longer perfectly on target; maybe your credentials section has to be tweaked or even completely rewritten. You may not feel up to this work and you may decide, against your better judgment, to stay with your current version of your book. However, this is exactly the right moment to make a major change and reposition your book so that it is more marketable—if the ideas you intend to communicate can be communicated in a more marketable version of your book.

You might reasonably ask, "Why wasn't I told to think about markets earlier, before I put so much time and effort into the current version of my book?" The answer is that a markets-first approach can easily lead to a book that is superficial and market driven. It was important that you begin by finding the book that was in your heart to write, not the book that appeared to be the most viable in the marketplace. If you do decide to make a large change, the new version of your book will be informed and enriched by all the work you have done up until now.

Now that you are very familiar with your core ideas, have written some chunks of your book, know something about the books that compete with and complement yours, and so on, you can make an informed decision about whether you want to stay with your original idea or make alterations that in your estimation will increase your book's readership. You are not obliged to make any changes in the direction of obtaining a wider readership, and in fact there is no guarantee that making such changes will produce a book that is more marketable than a book with a limited but easily targeted audience. If it is in your heart to stay with your current idea, by all means do so.

Let's say that the process of thinking about potential markets for your book hasn't caused you to make any significant changes to your book's frame or focus. Your next step is to brainstorm potential markets for your book, as I did with my creativity coaching book. Once you've identified those markets, you will want to describe them in rhetorically strong ways, using as many real facts and figures as you can muster. There are many rhetorical devices you can use to describe potential markets for your book. For example:

- *Who your readers are.* "My book on ocean rowing will be of interest to fitness-minded women in their twenties, thirties, and forties."
- *What they read.* "My book will be of interest to the three million combined readers of *Women's Fitness Magazine, Women Outdoors, Healthy Lifestyle,* and *New Woman.* It will be of particular interest to women who already read the leading rowing magazines, *Row Today,* with a circulation of 125,000, and *Ocean Rowing Digest,* with a circulation of 220,000."
- *What they listen to and watch.* "Interested readers also watch ESPN's weekly *Rowing Today* show, hosted by Marvin Smith, and ESPN-2's annual coverage of the Long Beach to Catalina Regatta, and listen to the nationally syndicated *Women's Health Today,* hosted by Sally Martin, and *Physical Woman,* hosted by Joan Jones."
- *Who they know.* "My book will be of interest to people who've adopted health guru Jane Jones's principles of lifetime fitness and who have purchased Mary Smith's *New York Times*–bestselling *Get Physical!*"
- *Where they go.* "My book will be of interest to the tens of thousands of spectators at ocean rowing regattas, to seaside visitors interested in adding ocean rowing to their vacation, to people who shop at Ocean Rowing Outlet and the Kayaks-R-You chain of boat stores, and more generally to women who work out in gyms and fitness centers, buy their clothes at Eddie Bauer, and regularly visit the *Physical Woman* website, which receives 10,000 hits daily."
- *What they join.* "The 5,000 members of the American Ocean Rowing Association and the 25,000 members of the International Federation of Ocean Rowers are likely readers, as are members of the Nau-

tilus Society, Independent Women in Sport, and Physical Women of America."

- *Who has a stake in the issue.* "Any woman who has been told that for health reasons she ought to get regular significant exercise would be interested in ocean rowing as a lifetime sport, so health newsletters, health publications, and websites like yourdoc.com and goodhealth.net would would want to publicize this information as a service to their readers and visitors."

Exercise : YOUR POTENTIAL MARKETS

Create the first part of your marketing and promotion section.

1. Brainstorm potential markets for your book. Do this brainstorming over a few days, so that markets that eluded you on the first day have a chance to surface.
2. Consider how you want to describe each of the markets you've identified.
3. Do whatever research is necessary to gain specific information about how many people make up each of these markets, what they read, what they watch, and so on.
4. Prepare enough drafts of your markets section so that you ultimately arrive at a rhetorically strong, convincing product.

WILLING YOURSELF TO MARKET AND PROMOTE YOUR BOOK

In the second section of your marketing and promotion section you will articulate how you can help market and promote your book. But before you begin to construct your sales plan you need to ask and answer in the affirmative the following question: Are you willing to identify yourself as a salesperson for your book and commit to marketing and promoting it?

Many writers aren't willing to commit to marketing and promoting what they write. There are any number of reasons why the marketing and promotions section of the book proposal is among the hardest for these authors to contemplate and create—because the territory feels foreign to them, because they are not aware that they are supposed to help sell their book, because, alternately, they are very aware that they are supposed to market their books and don't feel able to compete with authors more practiced at sales, and so on—but the main reason is that these authors are made anxious just thinking about promoting their books.

These fears are generally not within our conscious awareness. We do not realize or recognize that it is fear that's at the root of our lack of desire to think about how we might support our book. We say things to ourselves like, "I guess I can do interviews," or "I'll do interviews if I have to," but what we are actually thinking is, "I am scared to death of appearing before a million people as a putative expert and then coming off looking like an impostor. There is *so much* about my subject that I don't know—and of course those are *exactly* the things I'll be asked about."

Most writers fear public speaking—perhaps because of their introverted nature. Many of the writers I work with say specifically that they doubt they could talk intelligently about their book at book signings without fumbling and stumbling through the evening. They do not feel equal to representing their book in the world and would be thrilled if all they had to do was write and they could hire a proxy author, a real expert, to do the promotion. Yes, they know enough about ocean rowing to have written a book, but they don't know *everything* about ocean rowing. What if they're asked a question they can't answer? Yes, they've written a book about actors' business survival skills. But what if they're asked a question about an actor *they've never even heard of*? What will they do then? Won't they die on the spot?

These fears are out of all proportion to the actual threats involved, which makes them irrational. It is not only not the end of the world to flub a question while publicizing your book, it is no big deal. It is a trifling matter to give a less than stellar interview, to forget one of your book's main points, to look less polished than you had hoped to look. All writers have gotten a little egg on their face in the process of supporting their books and have managed to recover and reappear at their next interview or book signing. The reality of making mistakes and messes comes with this territory and must be embraced and accepted, not dreaded.

You may feel that you do not want to throw dollars at marketing your book and you may not have the dollars to throw. You may not even want to throw time and effort into promoting and marketing your book and you may decide that you might as well let your book proposal reflect that fact by providing a minimal sales section or no such section at all. You might even find yourself having a bit of an attitude about this part of the job—that is, "I wrote the thing; isn't it the publisher's job to sell it?"

The truth is, publishers will promote and sell your book, but you are the energy source who knows the most about your book's specific readership and, frankly, the one with the biggest emotional if not financial investment in making sure your book reaches that market. So while your publisher's publicity and marketing department will make sure to send review copies of your ocean rowing book to all the appropriate reviewers, you are the one who will be waking up at two a.m. with the initiative and energy to write personal letters to the directors of ocean rowing groups across the country.

In short, a top priority is that you *find the internal willingness to become a salesperson*. If you do, smart and reasonable marketing ideas will come to you as a matter of course and your ability to market and promote what you write will grow naturally.

$\mathcal{E}xercise$: WILLING YOURSELF TO SELL

Try to answer the following five questions.

1. Do you feel afraid to market and promote your book?
2. If you feel afraid, can you think about that fear head-on and try to change your mind?
3. Do you think that you shouldn't have to market and promote your book? Should sales be solely your publisher's responsibility?
4. If you hold that idea, can you think about it from a practical standpoint and change your mind?
5. Will you work to create the best marketing and promotion plan for your book that you can?

Take a full day to answer these questions. If you are stuck feeling as though you still don't want to market and promote your book, your reluctance will probably seriously harm your chances of selling your book. That reluctance will seep into every section of the book proposal and make it weaker than it would otherwise be.

When you find the willingness to promote yourself, your ideas, and your books, you give yourself an extra chance to get lucky with publication. Consider the following personal example. I was asked to contribute an article to a book. I did so and the book was published. Then I was asked if I would join a panel of contributors to speak about the book at a bookstore about 50 miles from my home. Given the traffic in my neck of the woods, that meant an hour-and-a-half commute. More important, I doubted that it would be a successful evening, since I suspected that we contributors had no recollection of the articles we had written the year before and that consequently we would provide a dull evening for the audience.

But I went anyway. I did this small marketing and promotion appearance for a book in which I had no financial investment because I believe it is my job to help market and promote my books, even those to which I am only a contributor. The evening began as I suspected it might, with the first few panel members declining to accept the microphone. I bit the bullet, took the microphone, and talked a bit. By the time I was done, other panel members had relaxed enough and recollected their articles enough to pick up the ball. The evening went well.

It turned out that the marketing manager for the publishing house who had published the book was in the audience. He went back and told people, "We have to do a book with Eric Maisel because he's a good public speaker." An editor from that house called me the next week and invited me to write a book for them. I wrote the book, which was short and a joy to write, and a producer from the Oprah show subsequently contacted my publicist and expressed some interest in having me appear on the program. My small participation ultimately had a big positive effect.

There's another lesson here. The book I was invited to write was the second in a series. The first book in the series had sold well, but its author had refused to market and promote his book, turning down interviews and declining book signings. So when his publisher wanted a new volume in the series, they were not inclined to return to this author. That was how it happened that I got the call.

I am not saying that Oprah will call if you give a talk at your local library to beef up your credentials or to support your book. But it will be harder for the gods of whimsy to spot you if you hide from them. They visit all the usual places: they read articles, they listen to interviews, they hear about you from someone who attended one of your talks. Won't you give the gods of whimsy a chance to spot you and choose you by going out and supporting what you write?

CREATING A MODEST, SENSIBLE, EFFECTIVE
MARKETING AND PROMOTION PLAN

If there were an infinite number of publishing slots, you would not need to come up with your own sales and marketing plan to include in your proposal. But the average large publishing house receives on the order of 10,000 queries and proposals a year—both unsolicited and via literary agents—and publishes a fraction of 1 percent of that enormous pile. You are competing for a scarce resource, a slot on a publisher's list, and since you *are* competing you must convince agents and publishers that your book is a better choice than the thousands of others they are considering.

Since you probably doubt that your marketing and promotion plan would impress anyone, you may find yourself saying to yourself, "Why propose anything at all? A lightweight plan will look silly next to the giant marketing plans I hear that other writers regularly propose. They say they are going to create their own book tour, buy back 10,000 copies of their book for sale at their workshops, and so on. What is the point of my saying that I have a website and a newsletter, given what other authors are saying?"

Do agents and publishers regularly see marketing plans full of big-ticket items? The answer is yes. Because authors have been told repeatedly by agents—either personally or in the books that agents write—that to be represented by an agent and to impress a publisher they must include in their proposal an impressive sales plan, they in fact do so (whether or not they mean what they are saying). For example, in the sample proposal that the literary agent Michael Larsen presents in *How to Write a Book Proposal,* the author he represents pledges to do the following things:

- She pledges to match the publisher's promotion budget.
- She claims she will purchase thousands of copies of her book for promotional purposes and resale (if she buys 2,000 copies a year for four years, that would cost her $50,000 or $100,000 alone).
- She says she will have 15,000 three-fold brochures printed at her own expense.
- She adds that she will hire a personal publicist (which might cost her as little as a few thousand dollars but is more likely to cost her $15,000 or $20,000 or even far more).
- Last but not least, she announces that she will make her own professionally produced promotional video to support the book.

Larsen informs us that this author received a nice six-figure advance for her book. *But she must have pledged in her proposal to spend two hundred thousand dollars of her own money at the very least.* This is disturbing news on two counts. First, a sales plan like this is our actual competition. Authors regularly make these grandiose pledges. Second, pledging such things apparently works, as Larsen's author did sell her book and did receive a large advance, presumably as much on the strength of her marketing plan as for any other reason. Even though editors are practiced at dismissing such overblown sales plans as so much hype, it is undoubtedly the case that plans of this magnitude do sometimes seduce editors into purchasing the book attached to the plan.

What should you do? If you are in the financial position and the frame of mind to market and promote your book on a grand scale, by all means say so. But you don't want to include big-ticket items in your marketing and promotion section merely because you think you are obliged to do so. Remember that publishers do know how to sell books and are not dependent on a writer's sales efforts. If they think that a book will sell, they will buy that book. The more an editor can picture in her own mind robust markets for your book and ways that her house can reach those markets, the less likely it is that she needs an over-the-top marketing plan from you.

Writers regularly interest editors in books that do not involve exceptional—or even modest—marketing and promotion plans. This may happen because the author is selling to a niche publisher who knows how to reach a specific audience, because the publisher is willing to take a chance on a fine book, because the author has a track record and a name, because the author has already published with that house and her book did well enough, and so on. There are many circumstances that allow for a book to be purchased even though its proposal has a limited marketing and promotion section.

Furthermore, whereas a percentage of guidebooks and literary agents are adamant that your proposal must have a very strong marketing and promotion plan, other agents do not require that of the writers they represent. They certainly advocate that a proposal be strong and that the book the proposal announces be marketable. But they do not demand that their authors make large claims and fill up pages with things that they might (but probably won't) do. It is possible to receive agency representation even if your proposal has a limited sales section.

The marketing and promotion plans that I put in my proposals are on the modest-to-nonexistent end of the spectrum. This has no doubt cost me sales and affected the sizes of my advances, with the largest hitting $25,000, but it hasn't prevented me from publishing. To piggyback on this point, one author who consulted with me did not include much of a marketing plan in her proposal and her book was sold at auction for $125,000. I never say in my proposals that I will hire a publicist, buy back books, create my own book tour, and so on, and that has not proved a death blow to my chances for publication.

What kind of marketing and promotion plan should you provide?

- A plan that you can visualize doing (allowing that you may have to stretch in some scary directions)
- A plan that demonstrates that you will exert energy on behalf of your book and that you don't expect your publisher to go to the ends of the earth on your behalf while you passively await publicity offers
- A plan that helps an editor visualize the markets for your book, especially ones that she might not contemplate on her own
- A plan that makes use of your strengths, connections, expertise, and experiences
- A plan that promises a few promotional tactics that may be new to you and still off in the future but that you are eager (or at least willing) to undertake
- A plan that uses language smartly

The following are some promises you might make that will feel legitimate to you, won't cost you too much, and will help make your case.

Indicate that you will do some advertising. Think through where your dollars might do the most good—today this is probably on the Internet. If you can find an online newsletter that goes out to 5,000 or 10,000 people who might be interested in your book and if advertising in that newsletter costs $100 or $200 an issue, that might be well worth offering. Your publisher might not have heard of or thought of this publication and might be reluctant to make even a small investment in something off the beaten path—but impressed that you would take on that small but potentially very effective task. You might say, "I will advertise *No More Dieting* in the *Fad Diet Newsletter,* which goes out to 10,000 subscribers." Another good place for your money is in trade magazine advertising, where ads aren't too expensive and will reach a highly targeted audience.

Start your own newsletter. Today, Internet resources make this very simple to do. Announce your newsletter to people interested in your subject and, when enough people have subscribed, send out your first newsletter. You might say, "I will announce *No More Dieting* in my monthly online newsletter, which reaches a targeted audience of individuals interested in the dangers of fad dieting."

Lead teleclasses (classes by phone). You can rent a phone bridge from various online sites for $20 an hour. If your class runs once a week for four weeks, your entire expense will be $80. You can advertise your teleclass in your newsletter, on the site where you rent the phone bridge, in chat rooms where people are talking about your subject, and so on. Even if only a few people sign up, you will make a small profit and you will be able to say that you lead teleclasses. You might say, "I will lead teleclasses based on *No More Dieting* on an ongoing basis."

Present at conferences. No matter what your subject is, you can craft a workshop that will be wanted at a conference somewhere. Identify the conferences you might reasonably present at, call or write for brochures from their past conferences, get a sense of how long their workshops last and what kinds of lectures and workshops presenters give, and create your talk. If eventually you actually do present, the cost to you would be the expense of travel and lodging (conference fees are usually waived for presenters), which might be anywhere from nothing for a local conference to $1,500 for a three-day conference three thousand miles away. You might say, "I will present at conferences, targeting the annual meetings of *Americans Against Fad Diets* and the *International Association for Healthy Eating.*"

These are just a few of the reasonable ideas that you might adopt. In books like John Kremer's *1001 Ways to Market Your Books* and Larsen's *Guerrilla Marketing for Writers* you will find additional ideas. There are also countless free electronic newsletters that specialize in marketing and promotion tips for writers. Want an example of excellent author participation? Donna Woolfolk Cross's efforts on behalf of her novel *Pope Joan* were exemplary. Cross called more than 350 reading groups on the telephone to discuss her book with them, often spending four or five evenings a week chatting with them. Her website, which she erected at her own expense, carried news of her telephone offer. In addition, she e-mailed information about her book to numerous organizations and spent $5,000 on targeted web banner ads. These marketing and promotion efforts helped the paperback edition of *Pope Joan* sell more than 100,000 copies in the United States and aided it in becoming an enormous bestseller in Germany, where it sold two million copies.

BIG-TICKET ITEMS

If you can financially afford to market and promote your book in a big way, you might want to say so. But be specific, so that your promises sound believable. Instead of saying "I will hire a personal publicist," do some research and say, "I will hire Mary Jones PR to help land me drive-time radio interviews in the major markets." Instead of saying "I will use one-third of my advance to help promote my book," pick a number you feel comfortable with and say "I will earmark $10,000 of my own money for marketing and promotion purposes." If you are interested in going this route, research these big-ticket items to learn which publicity firm to name, which cities to include on your self-created tour, how much it will cost you to produce your own brochures or promotional videos, and so on. It will probably take you several days to accomplish this research.

Think through whether or not you want to commit to any big-ticket items. If ultimately you choose to promise something large, lead with it in your sales plan.

Exercise : **DREAMING UP MARKETING AND PROMOTION IDEAS**

Spend some time over the next few days dreaming up many reasonable and useful things you can do to help market and promote your book. Try any of the following to help you generate your list of marketing and promotion ideas:

- Read one book on writers' marketing and promotion strategies.
- Attend one online writers' marketing and promotion workshop.

- Answer the question **What are 20 things I will do to market and promote my book?**
- Answer the question **What are 50 things I will do to market and promote my book?**
- Talk to writers you know about their marketing and promotion ideas and experiences.
- Join an online writers' group (there are thousands of them) and ask for suggestions about marketing and promoting your sort of book.
- Visit the websites of some well-known authors and send them each an e-mail inviting them to tell you one marketing or promotion idea that worked well for them.

Work on generating many marketing and promotion ideas. Then take your time and decide which of them you want to include in your sales plan, remembering that it will benefit you greatly to stretch and do things that right now may seem a little scary.

At this point, you are ready to put together this section of your proposal. Start by announcing the markets for your book and then lay out how you will promote your book, beginning with ideas that are most likely to impress or excite an editor. As with the other sections of the book proposal, you will have to produce multiple drafts of this section until it reads well and sounds convincing.

The time you spend on this section will reap you large dividends. In effect, you are teaching yourself how to market and promote your book at the same time that you are providing agents and publishers with the information they need. You are giving yourself a much-needed education. What you learn will help you sell your book once it is published—and will help you get it published.

Chapter 9

CREATING YOUR MAIN OVERVIEW, HEADLINE PARAGRAPH, AND BARE-BONES PROPOSAL

I n this chapter we look at three sorts of overviews of your book. The first is the main overview that opens your book proposal. The second is a single-paragraph overview that you can memorize and use to describe your book when you find yourself in a marketplace setting, say at a writers' conference. The third overview is a bare-bones book proposal that describes your book's highlights, including format and audience demographics, in a page or two and that can accompany your query letter when you query agents or editors about your book.

YOUR MAIN OVERVIEW

You start off your book proposal by presenting an overview of your project, usually in one or two pages. What you are selling, throughout the proposal and in the overview especially, is that you have a good idea for a book, that you have the right credentials to back up your idea, that there are readers for your book, that you will help your publisher reach these readers, and that your book makes sense in the context of other books published on this subject.

The overview is a snapshot of your nonfiction book project. It is always time-specific and reflects your current understanding of your project. The overview penned during the first week of thinking about your project, were you to craft one then, would probably bear little relation to the overview put together a month later, or six months later, or when the manuscript was completed—or, for that matter, a year after the book was published. Then your ideas would be influenced and altered by feedback from readers. If you wrote a new overview every month for the 12 months it took you to write the draft of your book, it's likely that each one would look different.

In fact, you might write your book's overview on three consecutive days and produce very different documents. This happens because your mind alights on one aspect of your book and focuses on it the first day, lands on another aspect the next day, and moves on to a third the day after that. On Monday I might craft an overview for this book that focused on the need for writers to put together an effective book proposal. On Tuesday it might occur to me that I had minimized the task of first arriving at a strong nonfiction book idea, so Tuesday's overview might lean in the direction of emphasizing that point. On Wednesday, partly as a reaction to Tuesday, I might decide to give both elements equal weight, explaining that this book would be about arriving at a good idea and also about producing a strong proposal.

Your three consecutive overviews might also differ dramatically because thinking about your book, as you would have to do in order to construct your overview, can cause you to change your mind about your book's shape or focus. On Monday, just as you finish constructing your overview for your book about coping skills for professional actors, a new principle might occur to you. On Tuesday, as you complete the overview that incorporates your latest principle, you might realize that your principles now fall into two rough groups, making it logical to divide your book into two parts. On Wednesday you have a brand new overview to write.

This many rewrites are probably in your future. But, as with any journey, you begin with a single step: writing your initial overview. Before you tackle that task, however, you'll want to devote some thinking time to the following strategic question: *Is there anything about my book idea, my credentials, my potential audience, or any other aspect of my project that might cause a literary agent or editor to object?*

START BY MEETING POTENTIAL OBJECTIONS

One important goal of the overview is to meet agent and publisher objections before they arise. As you think about this section of your proposal, you should be thinking about the sorts of objections an agent or editor might raise, for example that there is no market for your book, that reaching the markets that exist would be hard to do, that your book wants to do too many things at once, that your credentials feel too slight, and so on. Once you identify these potential objections, you can do one or another of three basic things:

1. *Change your book.* You might meet a potential objection by changing your book's approach, focus, or organization. For example, if you believe that an editor would say that your book has too small a market and suddenly you realize that this is a true and significant objection, you might broaden your approach to your idea before you did any more writing on it so that your book would have a chance of reaching a larger audience.

2. *Change your reader's mind.* You might endeavor to convince an agent or editor through your powers of selection, persuasion, and rhetoric that she should let go of her objection. That you can manage to change the opinion of an agent or editor once an objection has formed in her mind is actually quite unlikely. But if you *anticipate* the objection, you may be able to prevent it from ever arising as such in her mind. You might meet a potential objection before it arises by becoming more of an expert and beefing up your credentials section, by researching market demographics and presenting compelling numbers about potential purchasers of your book so as to make its markets clearer, and so on.

3. *Ignore the objection.* This path comes with three branches.

(a) You might accept that the objection would seem legitimate to some agents and editors but presume (and hope) that not every agent or editor will hold it as an objection. That is, you affirm that with the right agent or editor it won't *be* an objection. This means, of course, that you will need to find this right agent or editor and that you may have to suffer through many rejections that might be avoided if you met the potential objection.

(b) You might think about the potential objection and, having given it careful consideration, decide that it isn't really a problem. You may come to the conclusion that the thing you first suspected might be an objection really isn't one.

(c) You might act as if there couldn't possibly be any objections to your book and stick your head in the mud. This is not an approach with anything to recommend it.

In the first chapter of this book, I mentioned a writer who changed his book idea from *The Psalms and Celtic Spirituality* to a book called *The Road to Guazapa,* based on his experiences leading volunteer work brigades in Central America. He brainstormed potential objections to his new book idea and articulated how he would respond in order to meet these objections as follows.

Meeting Objections: *The Road to Guazapa*

OBJECTION 1: People are really not interested in Central America. Mexico, maybe, Costa Rica for its mountains, gorges, and tourist destinations, but Nicaragua or El Salvador? Not really.

RESPONSE: It is true that these countries are not tourist meccas. But this book is geared toward "armchair travelers": people who are looking for a cultural experience different from the tourist experience or from what they may have ever experienced themselves. The book will take readers inside a foreign culture, where they can experience a history far different from their own.

OBJECTION 2: The travel section of bookstores depends on selling books about travel destinations that people actually want to go to. My book would be out of place.

RESPONSE: One of the purposes of my book is to provide insight into a foreign culture. People browsing the travel section might say, "Hey, here's an interesting book to go along with *Lonely Planet* or *Fodor's* that would give me the flavor of Central America."

OBJECTION 3: My book is a hybrid. Some of it is about the peoples and cultures of Central America and some of it is about gringos on a goodwill mission. It doesn't fit neatly into a section of the bookstore.

RESPONSE: I see *Road to Guazapa* being placed in two sections of the bookstore: the travel section and the spirituality/religion section. The book fits in the spirituality/religion section because it contains inspiring stories of dedicated volunteers who travel to Central America to work side by side with natives to help improve the well-being of their communities. These volunteers are not Mother Teresas, but some of them are every bit as worthy of emulation.

OBJECTION 4: This kind of book has lots of good intentions, but it's not what people will buy. The topic only makes readers feel guilty that they are not doing more. It has a holier-than-thou flavor.

RESPONSE: The book does not preach that everyone should be on a mission to help the needy. The real surprise in this book is that the gringo volunteers end up receiving more from the native peoples than they could ever give. The ultimate discovery is that that through this cultural interchange everyone is enriched.

OBJECTION 5: When you write a book with vignettes, there is no plot, no adventure, nothing compelling to move the reader to want to turn the page.

RESPONSE: This is a good objection. I plan to format the book in such a way that readers follow the development of Seeds for Learning as it finds its way to becoming a vital, well-recognized social force in the communities where it works. In this way, readers will feel that they are taking part in the initial forays and will experience the obstacles, the setbacks, and, ultimately, the accomplishments.

This author used what he learned from this exercise of considering objections to make his overview stronger and more compelling than it might otherwise have been. He identified the idea that volunteers get more than they give as an important one and decided that saying this directly was the best way to begin his overview. He learned about the dramatic arc of his story, as volunteers experienced obstacles and setbacks but ultimately persevered, and concluded that highlighting this plot line was a powerful way to interest readers in his material. His work on meeting potential objections to his book benefited him when he sat down to create his overview.

Exercise : IDENTIFYING AND RESPONDING TO POTENTIAL OBJECTIONS

Identify potential objections to the book you are writing. Then decide how you want to respond to each objection. Try to be as concrete as you can in articulating how you will meet an objection. If you believe that you need to revision your book in order to meet a certain objection, say **how** you will revision the book. Rather than saying that you will become more of an expert, say **how** you will become more of an expert. If a potential objection to your business book for managers is that it seems very short, can you turn that into a positive by asserting that its brevity will be a boon to overworked managers who have little time left in the day to read? Try to identify how the results of this exercise can strengthen your overview.

WHAT MAKES FOR A STRONG OVERVIEW?

Now that you've done some work identifying and meeting possible objections to your book, let's take a look at a sample overview. I have deliberately chosen a somewhat flawed overview so that you can see the sorts of weaknesses a typical overview contains and what can be done to eliminate common mistakes.

A Blossom in the Brain
Overview 1

Much of the time that we grew up together, I hated my younger sister. As I lived in the shadow of her vitality and the violent absoluteness of her opinions, I struggled to define myself against her—and to defend myself against her. Besides which, I looked and sounded like her; many people couldn't tell us apart. By her late twenties she'd earned her law degree, and at 35 she took over my father's law practice. I was 39 and she was still not only my Achilles' heel but an Achilles' heel for my father, mother, and five other siblings.

Then, at 38, she was diagnosed with a malignant brain tumor. My family and I were responsible for taking care of a sister, both loved and feared, through her agonizing and prolonged death. Before her sickness, she had controlled my life through intimidation and then, just as I was struggling to find out who I was, she got sick and controlled my life through her illness.

My memoir chronicles a woman and her quirky, close family as they tried to come to grips with a sister over the three and a half years that she died, first losing short-term memory, then vision, then ability to tell forward from backward, then mobility. The book is organized chronologically around key events in her illness and my involvement in those events as friend, nurse, or foil.

It describes the conflict between intense and loving sisters who shared a passion for opera and country music, art and theater, and examines these passions to find clues about who they are and how they cope with disaster. For example, when Barbara loses her sight, I write about Impressionism and light.

The book delves into often unmentionable feelings: hatred of sister, hatred of self, fear of going blind, and fear of death in great specificity. Like Terry Tempest Williams's *Refuge,* it focuses on place and the attempt to find meaning in the experience of dying, but, unlike *Refuge,* contains significant conflict and humor.

Humans have always been both fascinated and fearful of the intricacies of the brain and attracted to and scared of having a loved one die at home. Both issues are considered in this memoir. As Mary Karr said, memoirs are popular today because people are fascinated by families. In this case, with a family that is irritable, quirky, close, and verbally dexterous, the advantage to the reader is that inner states, usually kept private, are made explicit.

Until I was 24, the distance of age and later geography meant I could ignore Barbara. Indeed, as the oldest, I saw myself as unconnected to my siblings in any significant way. I would go out in the world and find friends, work, a boyfriend. I would be a pleasant but distant older sister who gave nice Christmas presents and helpful instructions on life. At that point, I never guessed how strongly family would rule in my life nor how large an amount of time I would spend contending with my sister Barbara, even now, nine years after her death.

This overview is an appropriate length but doesn't make a strong impact for the following reasons:

We don't know what the book is about. Is it a book about two sisters or about an extended family? The author sometimes implies one and sometimes the other. Perhaps she is not confused in her own mind about the book's focus, but a reader can't be sure of the author's intentions.

It isn't clear that we will like the book's characters. The author puts us in some doubt that we will like her sister, who is presented as the family's Achilles' heel, and in doubt that we will like her or the rest of the family, since they sound more annoyed at the dying sister than concerned for her.

Many phrases lack clarity and rhetorical strength. What, for example, is a "quirky, close" family? Are we to think of an eccentric family out of Dickens, the television Addams family, a sinister family out of an Alfred Hitchcock movie, or what? Because we don't know and aren't clearly told, we have trouble picturing the author's family or caring about them.

Will the book be focused or will it wander? The author believes that mentioning that she will write about Impressionism and light enhances her proposal, but an editor is likely to worry that the book will be busy, jumping from idea to idea, and slowed down by the author's "beautiful" digressions. Does the author understand the principles of dramatic pacing and how to keep a reader's attention? We are not convinced that she does.

The overview is repetitious, hurting the author's chances on two counts. First, she is in danger of boring an editor, leading her to wonder if the finished product will also be boring. Second, she repeats ideas that were not clear to begin with. She talks early on about her close, quirky family and then later mentions her "irritable, quirky, close, and verbally dexterous" family, which is repetitious and again confusing.

She tells us that, "like *Refuge,*" her book is about "the attempt to find meaning in the experience of dying." However, as the central thrust of this memoir is almost certainly the love-hate relationship between two sisters, this comparison is *misleading and unhelpful.*

The last sentences are too leisurely and do not end the overview with a bang. The author spends three sentences telling us that she was disconnected from her family before her sister became ill. We would rather hear in some powerful, memorable way what she learned from the experiences that this memoir chronicles.

We haven't been told enough about the author. The job of the overview is to announce the complete package that you as an author are bringing to the table. If you're writing a book about rodeos and don't mention in the overview that you happen to be a rodeo champion, the overview isn't doing its job. So, too, with our author: we do not get enough about *her* in this overview, and she is as important to the project as her subject matter.

It will help the chances of the writer of this overview if she eliminates the ideas and sentences that do not help her make her case. It isn't always possible to know *why* a given sentence in your overview isn't effective, but if you suspect that a given sentence isn't strong or if you have a doubt about whether a given idea is a plus, rethink and revise the material in question.

If the author of this overview agreed with my assessment, then she would rewrite her overview, strengthening her case and subtracting any weak phrases and ideas. She would also add material about her qualifications and credentials. Of course she will get to talk about herself elsewhere in her proposal, primarily in her credentials section. But think about it. When would you like to know that the author who is proposing a rodeo book is a former national barrel jumping champion? One page into the proposal or 10 pages in? To hear that information early on gives the project a halo effect: it puts a smile in the reader's mind.

Many other things provide a similar halo effect: that you know the right people, that books of this sort always sell, that your subject is fresh rather than stale, that it has a larger audience than first meets the eye, that you are not just any author but a particularly energetic, savvy one, and so on. This information will appear elsewhere in your proposal in the appropriate places—the marketing and promotion section, the competing and complementary books section, the credentials sections—but a strategic sampling of it should appear in the overview as well.

Given these considerations, I would redo the overview we've been examining in the following way.

A Blossom in the Brain
Overview 2

Much of the time that we grew up together, I hated my younger sister. As I lived in the shadow of her vitality and the violent absoluteness of her opinions, I struggled to define myself against her—and to defend myself against her. By her late twenties she'd earned her law degree, and at 35 she took over my father's law practice. Then, at 38, she was diagnosed with a malignant brain tumor. Suddenly I became responsible for taking care of a sister, both loved and feared, through her agonizing and prolonged death.

Before her sickness my sister Barbara controlled my life through intimidation. Then, just as I was struggling to find out who I was, she got sick and controlled my life through her illness. *A Blossom in the Brain* explores that most unmentionable of feelings, hatred of a sister, and other powerful feelings as well: self-hatred, the terror of going blind, the horror of death at an early age. It describes a conflict examined in Greek and Shakespearean tragedy but rarely discussed in contemporary letters: the conflict between rival sisters. Unlike *A Thousand Acres,* in which sisters are pitted against one another but are defined against a man, their father, in *A Blossom in the Brain* two sisters are shown in direct, dramatic relationship.

I bring both psychological acumen and writing skills to this project. I possess a Master's in Social Work and a Master's in Creative Writing. I was director of training at a county Social Services office, I instructed supervisors nationwide on subjects like the effective use of authority and managing interdisciplinary teams, and, as a writing teacher, I've taught memoir writing to students at the University of Minnesota. I also have the presentation skills necessary to support *A Blossom in the Brain:* I have presented internationally and made scores of presentations on topics ranging from foster care planning to incest treatment. My skills as a writer, student of human nature, and presenter will help *A Blossom in the Brain* become a stand-out memoir.

A Blossom in the Brain examines the conflict between two intense sisters and their love-hate relationship. There are now tens of millions of educated professional women, the largest number in history, who think nothing of juggling work and family or tackling any professional challenge that comes their way. But how do they relate to each other? *A Blossom in the Brain* is the story of two contemporary women, blood rivals who must face their deep-seated differences as one ministers to the dying of the other.

I believe that this overview is stronger than the original one. However, it also announces a different book. In the original book we appeared to be getting two books in one, an intense interpersonal saga and a family drama. In my reworking of the overview, I focused exclusively on the interpersonal saga, reckoning that the "two sisters" theme was the real center of the book and also its most compelling feature. The author will have to decide what she thinks about this matter and will come to one of the following four conclusions:

- She may decide that her book is about her relationship with her sister, in which case this overview is accurate but her book needs rethinking.
- She may decide that her book is about both her relationship with her sister and her family's story but may make the calculated choice to let the overview focus like a laser on the two sisters theme because of its rhetorical power.
- She may decide that her book is about both her relationship with her sister and her family story and may feel compelled to get both of those themes into the overview, in which case she would need to add that second theme in a very strong, tight way to the overview.
- She may decide that the book is actually more about her family story than about her interpersonal relationship. If she goes in this direction, this overview will no longer represent her book and she will be compelled to write a new overview and rethink her book.

Exercise : **CREATING YOUR OVERVIEW**

Try your hand at writing your overview. Remember, the first overview you write will only be a draft. You'll have many revisions to do on it, both now and later. Keeping that in mind, I'd like you to sit down and create a first overview of your book. Over the next few days revise it as many times as necessary, until it effectively expresses your book's strengths and central ideas. When you are ready to send out your book proposal, revise your overview again so that it reflects your up-to-the-minute understanding of your book.

You want your overview to be as perfect as you can make it. No sentence in it should be lazy, no sentence in it should set off the wrong vibrations, no sentence in it should make an agent or editor think to herself "My, how late it's gotten!" It will take you many shots at writing the overview before you create one that effectively presents your ideas and highlights the strengths of your book. But if you make that effort and end up with a strong overview, you can congratulate yourself on having produced the single most important part of your book proposal.

There is only one rule when it comes to the overview: it must be effective. It doesn't matter if this section of your proposal is a paragraph long or three pages long. It doesn't matter if you repeat highlights from other sections of your proposal. It doesn't matter if your tone is playful or serious, fun-loving or matter-of-fact. All that matters is that a reader says to herself, "This is a good project. I like it."

YOUR HEADLINE PARAGRAPH

Your next task is to condense your overview even further into a single paragraph that does an effective job of presenting your book to the world. You may end up using this paragraph in a number of ways: as the literal first paragraph of your overview, as the opening paragraph of your query letter, as the explanation of your book that you give to agents and editors at writers' conferences, or as the way you speak to everyone you know about your book. You can think of this paragraph as your book's headline, sales pitch, summary paragraph, or opening gambit. Here are the opening gambit paragraphs for a few of the books I have been discussing.

For the ocean rowing book:

"People around the world know the rich rewards of single-scull ocean rowing. In *A Woman's Guide to Ocean Rowing* I plan to bring my 15-year expertise in this beautiful sport and my credentials as a champion rower to create a useful book that teaches experienced ocean rowers how to improve their skills and inspires a new audience of novices to try the sport for the first time."

For the actors' business survival guide:

"Many books have been written about the craft of acting and the lives of actors. But *Elephant and Rat: The Twelve Survival Skills of the Working Actor* is the first book to identify the actual business survival skills that actors need if they are going to succeed as working actors."

For the "two sisters" memoir:

"Much of the time that we grew up together, I hated my sister. A successful lawyer, she seemed destined for greatness while I was destined to stand in her shadow. But at the age of 38, she was diagnosed with a fatal brain tumor. *A Blossom in the Brain* is the story of the transformation of our relationship from one of hatred and rivalry to one of love and understanding."

Each of these headline paragraphs helps us quickly picture the book in question. Because literary agents and editors have to field innumerable book ideas, queries, and proposals, they will greatly appreciate the time you've taken honing your book idea down into one succinct paragraph. At the same time, the act of creating your headline paragraph will help you better understand your book and, by fixing its theme in your mind, keep your chapter summaries and sample chapter on track when you tackle those parts of the proposal.

Exercise : WRITE YOUR OPENING GAMBIT PARAGRAPH

Craft a single paragraph that succinctly captures what your book is about. After you've written a first draft of the paragraph, read it over. Does it precisely describe your book? Does it leave no doubt about the central idea you're communicating? If not, try again with another draft. Aim for no more than three sentences that crisply and powerfully describe your book. Keep refining and honing your paragraph until you are positive that it is both interesting and perfectly clear.

YOUR BARE-BONES BOOK PROPOSAL

You have now done enough work on your book proposal that you can put together a one- or two-page document, a kind of bare-bones "facts at a glance" book proposal, that serves you in a number of ways. First, the act of putting together this document helps clarify in your own mind what your book is about. Second, you can use this document to share your nonfiction book idea with friends and colleagues and to test it out in the world. Third, you can use it as an overview of your book to hand out to agents and editors when you meet them at conferences and workshops. Fourth, you can include it with your initial query letter to help explain your book.

Your bare-bones proposal should contain one or two sentences of explanation about the following crucial elements of your book:

- Idea, hook, or focus
- Format
- Author credentials

- Markets
- Proposal availability

The following is the bare-bones proposal that a writing client prepared before he went off to a writers' conference.

The Sportsman's Way
Taking the High Road in Sports
HOOK: A self-help *Profiles in Courage* for athletes, sports fans, and anyone interested in self-improvement.

This book does two things:
1. It gives inspiring true examples of sportsmanship.
2. It maps out an achievable ten-step program that anyone can use to become a better sportsman or sportswoman and a more self-confident person.

The Sportsman's Way is based on extensive research of true incidents of extraordinary sportsmanship worldwide and the author's lifelong involvement with sports, currently as the president of a company that organizes fundraising races.

Format: 70,000 words. *The Sportsman's Way* is composed of an introduction and conclusion and ten chapters, each approximately 5,000 words in length. Side quotes will accompany the text, with an exercise section at the end of each chapter.

MARKETS: Some special markets for *The Sportsman's Way* include readers of America's print magazines for running enthusiasts and track and field lovers, *Runner's World, Running Times, Northwest Runner, Running Journal, National Masters News,* and *Track and Field News,* as well as young hero-oriented readers of *Sports Illustrated for Kids.*

AUTHOR: Previously published in the *Christian Science Monitor, Eugene Register-Guard, U. S. Olympic Track and Field Trials Program and Newspaper.* Lifetime active athlete who has participated in sport from the recreational to college varsity level, passionately interested in sportsmanship since he stopped for a fellow competitor who had taken a wrong turn in a college cross-country race. Currently owns and directs athletic special events company San Francisco Running and Walking, whose clients include JPMorganChase, the San Francisco Giants baseball team, and numerous other professional trade associations.

PROPOSAL AVAILABILITY: Full proposal, including two sample chapters, currently available.

In addition to these basic categories, your bare-bones proposal might highlight your marketing and promotion ideas, your chapter titles, complementary books, or whatever you consider your project's strongest selling points.

Exercise : **CREATING YOUR BARE-BONES PROPOSAL**

To create your bare bones proposal, follow these steps:

1. Reread the sections of your book proposal that you've prepared so far—your main overview, your marketing and promotion section, your credentials section, your competing and complementary books section—and identify the strongest aspects of your project. Write these out on a separate sheet of paper.
2. Reread your accumulated notes on your book's central idea, its organizational scheme, its title and subtitle, and so on, and identify

key elements that make the case for your book. Note these down on a new sheet of paper.

3. Condense and strengthen the material you've identified as your project's strongest points into several short, crisp paragraphs or into a series of clear items suitable for a bulleted list.

4. Combine these short paragraphs or bulleted list items into a one- or two-page document that provides a clear and compelling overview of your book project.

Preparing these three overviews will have forced you to think hard about your book, identify its strengths and weaknesses, and better understand its central idea and organizational scheme. Having gained this clarity and with your book idea firmly in mind, you have reached an excellent moment to try to visualize how each chapter of your book will be organized and what it will contain in terms of ideas and actual content. As you will see in the next chapter, preparing your overview leads you to the next step in the proposal process: summarizing the unwritten chapters of your book so that readers of your proposal can picture your book from start to finish.

Chapter 10

CREATING YOUR CHAPTER SUMMARIES

An important section of your book proposal, often called the annotated table of contents, is composed of summaries of all of your book's chapters. How will you summarize chapters that aren't written yet and whose contents are poorly known to you—or even unknown? This sounds like a real fool's errand. But maybe it's a hero's adventure! There is nothing that stretches the mind more and makes better use of our imaginative faculties than thinking about things we want to exist that don't exist yet.

An inventor thinks about her invention in her mind's eye; then she gets cracking with real materials to see if she can bring her idea to fruition. A software programmer has a sense of what he wants his program to do and can even manipulate the program in his mind, but then he must turn his attention to codes and heuristics to make the program happen. The same is true with the chapters of your book. You will really know them only as and when you write them, but you can know a great deal about them before they are written.

You are about to imagine what each chapter of your book will contain. Your job is to summarize each of these chapters in a neat package as short as a line or two in length or as long as a few pages in length. Whatever its length, the job of this summary is to help agents and editors understand what each chapter of your book contains and to convince them that your book is built right and proper.

THE PROCESS OF SUMMARIZING
UNWRITTEN CHAPTERS

By this point you've jotted down many notes for your book and written several chunks of it. You probably possess notes and chunks for a few different versions of your book, since it probably morphed a few times as you attempted to wrestle your book into existence. If you did the exercise on page 65 called "Imagining Versions of Your Book along the Secular-Existential Continuum," you've even produced a few different tables of contents. In the following exercise you'll have the opportunity to settle on one working table of contents for the current version of your book. You will then work from this table of contents when you move on to the next step of envisioning and writing a brief summary of your book's chapters.

Exercise : **CREATING YOUR TABLE OF CONTENTS**

1. Read over the notes you've made so far, including your exercise responses, your draft overviews, and any rough tables of contents you've produced already.
2. Using your notes and your current best thinking about your book project, prepare a table of contents. For certain books this may be

a simple procedure where, in a few seconds' time, you create a straightforward table of contents. For example, you may decide to organize your cookbook in a traditional way and have one chapter cover fish dishes, another cover chicken dishes, and so on. Or your self-help book may be organized around 12 steps or secrets and naming the steps or secrets turns out to be a rapid affair.

On the other hand, you may be writing a creative nonfiction book like a memoir and find that you are having a much harder time envisioning what your book will contain, how it will be organized, and, consequently, what its table of contents will look like. Here, too, though, you will want to try to comprehend the scope and contents of your book and arrange those contents in manageable chapters. For now your chapter headings may be only rough place-markers, like "the train ride from Wichita with my mother," "arriving in Burbank," "mother meets the movie producer," and so on.

3. Double-check the table of contents you just created and think about whether it seems reasonable and logical.

Once you know your book's table of contents, you are ready to summarize the unwritten chapters of your book. The first step is to build up your notes for each chapter as described in the following exercise. This will entail figuring out whether a morsel you intended to include somewhere in your book should go in chapter 3 or chapter 7, deciding whether the problems you envision with chapter 5 might be remedied by some strategic research, and so on. Each chapter will have its own life, its particular strengths and weaknesses, and its own special character.

Exercise : INVESTIGATING YOUR UNWRITTEN CHAPTERS

1. Head a separate sheet of paper with the name of each of your book's chapters. For each chapter, use these sheets to record your answers to the following questions.

- What do I intend to say in this chapter? What material will I be covering?

- Of the things that I intend to say, which do I consider the most important?

- How will I highlight these important points? For example, will I begin the chapter with one of them and end the chapter with another one, or use each as the focal point of a subsection of my chapter?

- How will each chapter be designed? Am I dividing each chapter up into a certain number of subsections and using the same number of subsections for each chapter? Does each chapter represent a specific length of time, a single event, a different aspect of an ongoing metaphor?

- What material might I include in the chapter to meet potential objections to my book? For example, if my book as a whole feels short on drama, can I add controversial material, conflict, or suspense to this chapter?

- What additional research, if any, will writing this chapter require?

2. Read over the notes you just produced. Then attempt to answer the following questions for each chapter:

- How does the chapter begin?
- What major elements does the chapter include?
- How does the chapter end?

3. Take a few hours or a day off and then return to your notes. Try to answer the following questions about each chapter:

- Does the concept of the chapter feel strong?

- If not, what would make it stronger? For example, is it too slight and in need of more material? Is it too long and in need of trimming or division into two chapters? Does it contain a lot of disparate material and need restructuring and refining?

Continue working with your notes over the course of several days until you feel that each chapter is well known to you and as strong as you can currently make it.

Note: if you've had trouble with this exercise, it may be because your book isn't solidly organized yet. You may want to reread the first four chapters of this book, which are intended to guide you to a focused book idea, repeat some of the exercises you completed earlier, or try a few of the exercises that you skipped the first time around. If you still can't figure out what your book is actually about, it may be that you can only know your book by writing it. In this case, working through a proposed table of contents and summarizing your chapters simply won't work for you. You will need to prepare a schedule for actually writing your book and sit down to do just that. Commence writing your book and set a date a month or two hence to check in with yourself to see if writing your book straight through continues to feel like the right choice.

Once you have a good sense of what your book's chapters will contain, you are ready for your next task: deciding what method you will use to summarize your unwritten chapters.

TWELVE TECHNIQUES FOR SUMMARIZING

You have a choice of several ways by which to summarize your chapters. The following are twelve techniques you can use to build your chapter summaries. As I name them I'll provide you with examples and identify some strengths and weaknesses of each one. (When I say that a method has a certain weakness, I will usually mean that it has this weakness only if used by itself to summarize a given chapter. When used in conjunction with another method, the weaknesses of each are typically minimized.)

Twelve techniques for summarizing:

1. Announcing an outcome
2. Identifying what questions your chapter answers
3. Using a bulleted list
4. Producing a summary paragraph or paragraphs
5. Producing a summary paragraph directed at an end reader
6. Announcing a chapter highlight
7. Identifying a central point and providing examples
8. Paralleling your chapter model
9. Including an excerpt from the chapter
10. Producing a narrative chapter summary
11. Producing a comprehensive chapter summary
12. Mixing and matching

Let's take a look at these techniques in detail.

1. *Announcing an outcome.* In this method, you announce what your chapter intends to accomplish by using the rhetorical phrase, "By the end of this chapter you will learn . . ." The strength of this method is

that by providing a simple headline for your chapter, you avoid confusing a reader and overloading her with too much information. Headlines of this sort tend to be rhetorically compelling, just as a newspaper headline like "War Declared!" or "Stock Market Soars!" is compelling. The mind appreciates simplicity and statements that feel as if they come with an exclamation point attached.

The author of the hypothetical book about the business survival skills of actors called *Elephant and Rat* might announce an outcome for his "building the hide of an elephant" chapter in the following way:

By the end of this chapter you will have learned how to build a skin as thick as an elephant's to protect you when you deal with talent agents, casting directors, artistic directors, producers, the media, and the public.

Other examples:

By the end of the chapter, readers will be able to bake baguettes as good as any you can find in France.

By the end of the chapter, readers will know how to create a budget that takes into account their fixed expenses, their discretionary spending, and their short- and long-term life goals.

The weakness of this method is that an outcome statement often doesn't include much real information. It may excite a reader's ear to know that by the end of the chapter she will be able to bake a terrific baguette, but when she stops to think about it she will realize that she has no clue what is actually in the chapter. This may make her wonder if you do. If your credentials are so strong that it goes without saying that you must know what this chapter will contain, a headline or out-come statement may work. But if you must convince an editor that you know what you will be writing about, an outcome statement may be too skimpy evidence of that knowledge.

2. *Identifying what questions your chapter answers.* In this method, you announce that your chapter will answer one, two, or three impor-tant questions. The strength of this method is that, like the outcome statement or chapter headline, this device has the rhetorical strengths of simplicity and clarity. A reader is likely to feel that she has gotten a good sense of what your chapter's theme or themes will be.

For example:

In this chapter of *Elephant and Rat,* I answer the following ques-tions: why actors need to acquire the skin of an elephant if they are going to survive in the acting business, what techniques you need to master in order to acquire a thick skin, and how you can effec-tively balance necessary vulnerability with equally necessary invul-nerability.

Here is another example:

This chapter answers the question that will be on a reader's mind after our mutual funds discussion in the previous chapter: If there is no difference in performance between no-load funds and loaded funds, why would anyone choose to buy a fund with a load?

The weakness of this method is that a reader is unlikely to feel that he knows what the chapter's contents will be or whether the writer will actually arrive at answering the questions she claims she will answer. If the writer has otherwise convinced a reader that she will deliver good contents in each chapter, this will be less of a drawback. But if the reader is not certain that the writer can and will deliver, then this minimalist approach will not work so well.

3. *Using a bulleted list.* In this method, you list several of the topics that your chapter will cover. The strength of this method is that a bulleted list allows you to list disparate things that do not necessarily connect and that may be hard to connect when you actually write the chapter. It is also a tried-and-true method of summarizing a chapter that you have outlined a little but don't really know very well.

Here's an example:

In chapter 3 you will learn:
- Why it's important for actors to acquire the hide of an elephant in their business dealings
- Several different methods for acquiring a thick skin
- How three actors in repertory theater suffered professionally from being too thin-skinned to handle competition
- How to effectively balance vulnerability and invulnerability
- One tried-and-true method for "putting on your elephant's hide" just before interviews, auditions, and callbacks

The weakness of this method is that bulleted points are islands of ideas and as such often don't feel connected and don't resonate too well with the reader, who has the feeling that she sort of has an idea what the writer has in mind but not any concrete understanding. This is no problem if a publisher or agent is already on your side, for then she will say to herself, "I think this sounds okay." But it is a problem if you are trying to move a reader to your side. Bulleted lists are a decent shorthand when two people are on the same page, but they don't really fire a reader's imagination or help her fall in love with what you're proposing.

Long bulleted lists also raise the suspicion that you are trying to do too much in the chapter, which leads inexorably to the thought that you don't know your chapter well and are producing a laundry list of things that might go into the chapter. Conversely, a very short bulleted list will make the chapter feel skimpy and make the reader say to herself, "Is that all there is?"

4. *Producing a summary paragraph or paragraphs.* In this method, you write one or two paragraphs in which you objectively summarize what your chapter will contain. The strength of this method is that a straightforward summary paragraph in which you identify your chapter's main points tends to be neat and logical. It also can, despite its brevity, feel quite complete, especially when used in conjunction with a short bulleted list, an excerpt, or some other add-on device. It is a businesslike method that can do an excellent job of summarizing your chapter, just so long as every sentence in the paragraph does good work.

Here's an example:

In chapter 3, readers are led step-by-step through the process of acquiring the thick skin of an elephant. Through interviews with three well-known actors, readers are reminded how important it is to acquire defensive skills and to effectively handle criticism and rejection. Several exercises help readers practice building a thick skin, including one exercise that teaches them how to put on and take off their thick skin in under 60 seconds. By the end of the chapter readers will know when they should protect themselves and when they should remain vulnerable and will possess an array of strategies for effectively competing in the marketplace.

The main weakness of this approach is that it can sound rather distant and impersonal, which means that it may not inspire much enthusiasm for your book. Second, its brevity, which is a plus for a busy reader, is also its weakness, as it may not convey quite enough information to assure an agent or publisher that you have a strong plan for your chapter and a real understanding of its contents.

5. *Producing a summary paragraph directed at an end reader.* In this method, you address the reader of your book as if he or she were an intimate. The main strength of this approach is that it can be both personable and passionate. This can be an excellent way to summarize chapters in self-help and how-to books and can be used for any other kind of book as well.

Here's an example:

You've probably found yourself at auditions, callbacks, and interviews wishing that you could just disappear and not have to deal with the criticism and rejection that you know are coming. These feelings prevent a lot of actors from entering the marketplace often enough or giving their best effort when they do audition. What can really help you with these feelings is acquiring a thick skin, a metaphorical layer of protection over your emotions that is as thick as an elephant's hide, so that you feel protected whenever you enter the marketplace. In chapter 3 we explore, through interviews and exercises, why it's so important that you acquire a thick hide in your business dealings.

The weakness of this method is that a single paragraph, no matter how intimate or personable, can't do the job of proving to a prospective agent or publisher that you really know what your chapter contains, that it contains enough, that it contains the right things, and so on. But if you combine this "for the reader" paragraph with other devices, like a bulleted list or a chapter excerpt, you can avoid this problem.

6. Announcing a chapter highlight. In this method, you focus like a laser on some interesting, exciting, or unusual aspect of your chapter. It is an extremely useful method when you don't really know what your chapter will contain but feel confident that you know what *a part* of it is about. You call that part a "highlight" and describe it in detail, letting the fact that you're not covering anything else evaporate through your use of rhetoric. If your highlight works, the reader is likely to believe that you can handle the rest of the chapter equally well.

Here's an example:

In chapter 3 we examine why actors must protect themselves in their business dealings by developing a "thick skin." A highlight of this chapter is an interview with the legendary actress Bernadette Smith, star of the Berkeley Repertory Theater for 30 years. Smith reveals for the first time that she never ventured to New York or Hollywood until she became well known for her repertory roles as Medea and Blanche because she felt too vulnerable to compete in those highly competitive markets.

The weakness of this method is that providing a highlight doesn't really summarize your chapter. If the reader is concerned that your chapter contains too much, too little, or not the right stuff, her doubts will not be assuaged by a highlight. But providing more information, say in a bulleted list, might help in this regard.

7. *Identifying a central point and providing examples.* In this method, you identify the central point you intend to make in your chapter and announce how you intend to illustrate that point by describing a few examples. The strength of this method is that the mind likes to be provided with a main idea and examples (three examples are generally the right number). Because the mind likes this kind of presentation, it has rhetorical strength and works well as a means of summarizing chapters that in fact are organized around a main idea and examples.

Here's an example:

In chapter 3, three well-known repertory theater actors describe how they consciously worked to develop a thick skin to help them succeed at the business end of acting. Bernadette Smith shares with readers a guided visualization she created and dubbed "nobody home," which she used to land a pair of national commercials. John Hightower describes the moment, when he lost his temper at an important callback, that he first realized that he had to detach from the audition process and not take personally what casting directors had to say to him. Barbara Adams walks readers through her process of what she calls "building armor," a process she goes through every time she auditions for a role.

The weakness of this method is that if your chapter includes more than a single idea and some examples, then you are not actually summarizing it using this method. And many book chapters will not lend themselves to being summarized in this fashion.

8. *Paralleling your chapter model.* If you've decided that each chapter in your book will be organized in a similar way around a chapter model and you have explained that in your proposal, then you can summarize your chapters by paralleling that model. The strength of this method is that it is neat, clean, and logical. The reader will be able to picture each chapter and will feel quite convinced that she knows what you are offering. Indeed, if you employ this method of summarizing you will be practically writing your book as you go.

Here's an example.

Chapter 3 is organized as follows:

1. I identify and describe the central skill of the chapter: in this case, acquiring a thick skin.

2. I present two exercises, one called "Thickening Your Hide," which helps readers begin to acquire this needed emotional armor, and a second called "How Thick a Hide Should You Grow?" that helps them create a skin that is thick enough to protect themselves but not so thick that they come across to prospective employers as defensive, distant, or disinterested.

3. I include portions of my interviews with three well-known repertory theater actors. Bernadette Smith explains her methods of maintaining a thick skin while also remaining vulnerable enough to feel. John Hightower talks about how he had to grow an elephant's hide to deal with everything from mercurial guest directors and hysterical costumers to drunk leading ladies and audiences you could number on one hand. Barbara Adams walks readers through her process of what she calls "building armor" that she goes through every time she auditions for a part.

4. I discuss the shadow side of invulnerability and explain why actors must build a thick skin in their business relationships but remain vulnerable enough to feel when they act.

5. I present a final exercise that helps actors thicken their skin in under 60 seconds, an exercise they can use before auditions and other marketplace interactions.

The weakness of this method of presentation is that it is a little on the static and mechanical side and can become boring. But if you take care to make each of your points clear and interesting, this problem can be minimized, and this method of summarizing may prove an excellent one.

9. *Including an excerpt from the chapter.* In this method, you use a chunk that you've written to give the reader the flavor of the chapter. The strength of this method is that an excerpt, because it is an actual part of the chapter, makes us feel that the chapter has a certain reality and substance. It encourages us to believe that the writer knows what her chapter will be about and gives us the sense, perhaps unjustified, that we too know what the chapter will be about.

Like the highlighting method, this method of summarizing is very useful when you have an excellent excerpt that you know will make a good impression. For example, with respect to the chapter I've been discussing, the author might include several strong paragraphs from his interview with Bernadette Smith in his summary of that chapter.

One weakness of this method is that if you do not employ excerpts in your other chapter summaries, it will seem a little strange that you included an excerpt in this chapter summary. It may make your reader wonder if this is the only good material in your book. Therefore you may be forcing yourself to include excerpts in all of your chapter summaries if you include an excerpt in any one.

10. *Producing a narrative chapter summary.* In this method, you de-scribe your chapter in detail over the course of several paragraphs, pro-ducing a half-page to one-page narrative description of your chapter. The strength of this method is that it can do a very nice job of com-municating how you write, how you think, and what the thematic concerns of your chapter will be. It may be the best way to communi-cate your writing style and your ability to tell a story.

Here's an example.

Chapter 3 opens with the question "Why do actors need to acquire a thick skin if they are to survive in the business?" Several reasons are provided, and actors are helped to realize that much of what they customarily take personally in their interactions with casting directors, artistic directors, and producers is better dealt with in a cool, detached, impersonal manner.

Two exercises are provided to help readers acquire the thick skin they need. Readers are taught a guided visualization in which they initially picture themselves unprotected in their business dealings and then protected, and then they explore a technique they can use to vary the thickness of their skin according to cir-cumstances.

Readers also learn lessons about self-protection from three well-known repertory theater actors. Bernadette Smith discusses the psychological relationship between actors and directors. John High-tower explains how he grew a tough emotional skin to help him deflect everything from hysterical costumers to drunk leading ladies. Barbara Adams walks readers through a preaudition process that she calls "building armor."

The next section offers five strategies for balancing vulnerability and invulnerability. Actors must access their feelings if they are to act genuinely, so a thick skin is not an asset on stage. At the same time, a thick skin may be needed on stage to deal with dictatorial directors, grandiose costars, the chaos and conflicts of rehearsal periods, and so on.

The weakness of this method is that it may provide the reader with more information than she wants, taxing her or boring her in the process. But if you pare your narrative summary down to its essentials and write in a lively style that holds the reader's interest, this method can prove an excellent one.

11. *Producing a comprehensive chapter summary.* In this method, you lay out your chapter in even greater detail than with the previous method, carefully articulating what your chapter contains. The obvious strength of this method is that you are providing the reader with a lot of information and also learning a great deal about your book in the process. Were you to produce comprehensive summaries for each of your chapters, you would be providing your reader with the best possible understanding of what your book is about. You would also have come a long way toward completing your book.

The primary weakness of a comprehensive summary is that it is likely to tax a busy agent or editor's patience. If you trust your material and your ability to present it compellingly, providing an agent or editor with comprehensive summaries will provide the best idea of what your book includes. But you might also consider the possibility that "less is more." While this method provides an author with an excellent understanding of her book, it is likely to produce more material than an agent or editor will want to read.

12. *Mixing and matching.* If you produce a comprehensive chapter summary, you obviously do not need to say anything more about that chapter. But if you use any of the other methods I've described, you may find that it alone isn't sufficient to convey what your chapter is about or doesn't seem compelling enough by itself. In that case, try a summarizing paragraph combined with a bulleted list, a model chapter summary combined with an excerpt, or some other combination that effectively presents your chapter. For example, if you combined the intimacy of method 5 (writing as if you were speaking to the end reader) with the rhetorical strength of method 6 (announcing a chapter highlight), you would produce a two-paragraph chapter summary that does a good job of presenting this chapter, as follows.

You've probably found yourself at auditions, callbacks, and interviews wishing that you could just disappear and not have to deal with the criticism and rejection that you know are coming. These feelings prevent a lot of actors from entering the marketplace often enough or giving their best effort when they do audition. What can really help you with these feelings is acquiring a thick skin, a metaphorical layer of protection over your emotions that is as thick as an elephant's hide, so that you feel protected whenever you enter the marketplace. In chapter 3 we explore, through interviews and exercises, why it's so important that you acquire a thick hide in your business dealings.

A highlight of this chapter is an interview with the legendary actress Bernadette Smith, star of the Berkeley Repertory Theater for 30 years. Smith reveals for the first time that she never ventured to New York or Hollywood until she became well known for her repertory roles as Medea and Blanche because she felt too vulnerable to compete in those highly competitive markets.

Exercise : SUMMARIZE YOUR CHAPTERS

You are now ready to summarize the unwritten chapters of your book. The steps are:

1. Gather the notes you produced earlier for the "Investigating Your Unwritten Chapters" exercise.
2. Decide what method you will use to summarize your chapters.
3. Summarize one or two chapters and decide if the summarizing method you've chosen seems effective. If the first style you've chosen doesn't seem to work, try again with another style. Continue this process until you find the best summarizing method for your book.
4. Summarize your book's chapters using the method you've chosen. Periodically evaluate whether your chosen style continues to be effective for every chapter. If at some point it doesn't, try another style and continue the process until all your chapters are effectively summarized in a consistent style.
5. Every so often step back and evaluate whether your table of contents still makes sense. Do you need additional chapters? Fewer chapters? A new organizational scheme? If so, stop everything and make the changes you deem necessary.
6. Polish each chapter summary until it shines.
7. Collect your chapter summaries into a section you call "Chapter Summaries" or "Annotated Table of Contents." Include this section in the appropriate place in your finished book proposal.

EVALUATING YOUR BOOK AND MAKING ANY NECESSARY CHANGES

Once you've completed your chapter summaries, step back and evaluate your book as a whole. For probably the first time since the idea for it popped into your head, you now have a clear idea of what your book will cover, what will be left out, how it will be organized, and a sense of its strengths and weaknesses. This is an excellent moment to ask yourself whether you are happy with your book's focus, shape, and contents and to decide what, if any, changes you might want to make.

If you have changes to make, bite the bullet and make them now. It will pay real dividends to make use of what you've learned as you summarize your book's chapters to alter and strengthen your book. Even if these changes entail a lot of work, go ahead and make them. Approach any revisioning you deem necessary as optimistically and energetically as you can, secure in the knowledge that you are doing what is necessary to bring a good book into existence.

CREATING YOUR SAMPLE CHAPTER

Now that you've summarized your book's chapters, written your overview, compared your book to other books in your subject area, and tackled the other tasks that comprise thinking a nonfiction book into existence and building a book proposal, several steps remain before you are ready to submit your book proposal to literary agents or editors. In this chapter we'll look at three of these remaining steps:

1. Writing a sample chapter (or chapters).
2. Determining your book's length.
3. Calculating when you'll be able to deliver your completed manuscript.

STEP 1: WRITING YOUR SAMPLE CHAPTER
OR CHAPTERS

Almost all book proposals come with at least one sample chapter and some come with more than one. If you are not an already published author, it is hard to imagine literary agents and editors considering your proposal if it doesn't contain a sample chapter that shows them how effectively you write and that reveals how you intend to convey the content of your book. One of my clients, who received a $325,000 advance for a diet book, was still asked by her publisher for a sample chapter when she proposed a sequel.

Publishers need to be sure that you can deliver what you promise. While you may be unhappy with the idea of writing a whole chapter without any guarantee that your book will ultimately interest agents or publishers, you're still going to have to do it. Therefore you might as well commit to the idea. But you *do* have the choice of which chapter of your book you will write and submit as a sample. Just as you endeavored to include strategic information about the value of your book and your strengths as a supporter of your book in your credentials section, in your marketing and promotion section, and elsewhere throughout your proposal, your choice of which chapter to write is a strategic one. You don't want to choose the chapter you suspect will be the most enjoyable to write or the quickest to write. Rather, you want to choose the one that will best garner the interest of agents and publishers.

Upon what criteria will you base this strategic decision? Say that you are writing a self-help book for women recovering from heroin addiction. Chapter 1 seems like the most logical one to submit as your writing sample, since you've planned that it will introduce your subject. But you've also decided that you will outline your self-help recommendations in chapter 2, so that chapter also seems very important to show. Then there's chapter 3, where you share some excellent vignettes and powerful anecdotes and bring your material to life. Wouldn't that be a smart one to choose? And what about your last chapter, where you intend to tie everything together? Wouldn't it impress an editor to see how effectively you do that integration?

Which of these chapters should you choose to write? If there are no overwhelming reasons to choose otherwise, you should choose the first chapter. This may be the introduction, if your book has a hefty introduction that amounts to a real chapter, or the chapter that follows the introduction, if the introduction is brief and perfunctory. Your first chapter, if it is done well, will effectively introduce the reader to your subject matter and is therefore the most logical choice for your sample chapter.

However, there may be compelling reasons for not choosing the first chapter as your sample. The primary one is that your first chapter may be merely a summary of the information in your chapter summaries. This is very helpful for the ultimate reader of your finished book, who won't see your chapter summaries, but in a book proposal it amounts to useless repetition. If your first chapter rehashes or restates your chapter summaries, you won't be providing the reader of your proposal with new information, and you may come across as lazy and inconsiderate of the reader's needs.

There's a second reason to be careful about choosing the first chapter of your book as the sample chapter in your proposal. Often a book's first chapter is a vague and disjointed affair because a writer is using that chapter to familiarize *herself* with her material. This leads to a lot of hemming and hawing and beating around the bush. Because she doesn't yet have a clear picture of what meaning she intends to make, she temporizes in the first chapter and doesn't really get going until chapter 2, when all the preliminaries are behind her.

If you have serious doubts about choosing your introduction or first chapter as your sample chapter, how will you determine which of the other chapters to select? A good choice would be one that does an excellent job of showing off your knowledge and expertise. Read down your table of contents and make note of your internal response to each of the chapters listed there. "Don't really know what that one's about," you may think about your chapter 2. "Don't really know what that one's about," you might say about chapter 3. But when you get to chapter 4, you might find yourself thinking, "Boy, do I know what goes into *that* one." That is a good chapter to write for your proposal. First, you will be proving to a reader that you know something. Second, you will do less hemming and hawing in that chapter, since it is ready to be filled up with material on the tip of your tongue. Third, you will bring a certain vitality and enthusiasm to a chapter that makes use of what you know so well.

What this means, however, is that you are showing the reader of your proposal an atypical chapter: that is, one that may be better and richer than your other chapters might conceivably be. This may be a problem down the road, unless you make a firm pact with yourself that you will learn whatever it is you need to learn and do whatever it is you need to do to make all the other chapters as good as your sample chapter. By all means show your strongest chapter, but register the fact that your book's other chapters may need considerably more time and effort than your sample chapter did.

You may choose a sample chapter to write, write it, and find that it isn't as strong as you had hoped. In that case, you will have to revise it until it is strong or, if it can't be strengthened at this time, write another chapter to use as your sample. Similarly, you may discover that your sample chapter is fine but doesn't do a good enough job of selling your book, perhaps because it is too short or not really representative of your book as a whole. In that case, use it as a sample but submit another chapter as well. Do not accept that your sample chapter or chapters are right until they *are right,* since this sample is vital to the success of your project.

Exercise : CHOOSING YOUR SAMPLE CHAPTER

1. Study your annotated table of contents. With regard to each chapter in your book, ask yourself the following three questions:

- Would this chapter do an excellent job of communicating my book's central idea?

- Would this chapter convince a reader that my book is strong and compelling?

- Do I have the feeling that I know a lot about this chapter and that I might be able to fill it with lots of good material?

2. If you answer yes to all three questions for a particular chapter and find that you can't for any of the others, that chapter is the logical choice to write for your book proposal. If you can answer yes to all three questions for several chapters, congratulations! You can choose any one of those chapters to write and may base your choice on your enthusiasm for a particular chapter or for some strategic reason (e.g., because it includes an anecdote that you feel will have an emotional impact on a reader). Remember that, all things being equal, the nod should go to your introduction or first chapter.

3. If you can't answer yes to these three questions with respect to any of your chapters or you just aren't sure, one way or the other, try to gauge your reaction to each chapter and select the one that comes closest to meeting these criteria. If a few chapters come close, select the one for which other strategic reasons like those mentioned earlier exist.

4. Sleep on your choice. If it still seems like the proper choice the next day, commit to writing it as the sample chapter for your book proposal.

As you weigh the pros and cons of your various unwritten chapters as potential sample chapter choices for your proposal, you may well become convinced that you should write *all* of your book's chapters, then decide which one or ones to submit. What could be the problem with traveling this route? In theory, nothing at all. Writing several chapters of your book, or even the whole book, and then choosing one or more chapters to use as a sample in your proposal is certainly a logical idea.

But psychologically and practically there are certain problems. As a practical matter, this process will delay the submission of your proposal for a significant amount of time, since it will take you many months or even a year or two to write your book. In addition, once you have several or all of your chapters completed, you may be tempted to send out more of your manuscript than an agent or publisher is willing to read. The bigger problem is that as you try to write your book, you may become blocked and decide to put your book aside indefinitely. Therefore, the safest course is to choose a single chapter (or perhaps a couple) to write.

Once you've decided which chapter you intend to write, there are two basic approaches to writing it:

- In the first approach, you reread your chapter summary and the notes for the chapter you've chosen as your sample, then you plunge ahead, writing and thinking, thinking and writing, until a draft of your sample chapter is completed. In this approach you forgo making decisions about your chapter's length, structure, or contents beforehand and instead make those decisions as you write and when you revise.

- In the second approach, you step back and view your chapter as part of a whole. You decide what each chapter will contain and, consequently, what this chapter contains. You then outline your chapter, either in a rough way or a detailed way, and then write the chapter according to that outline.

There are pluses and minuses to each approach. The first approach allows you to get deep into your material and make discoveries about your chapter and your book that you might not make if you began by structuring and outlining. But you run the risk of producing mountains of material, sending your book off in an unintended direction, or creating a chapter that requires a lot of revising and revisioning. To take just one example of how this might play itself out, you might write at great length about your subject (since you're probably writing a chapter about which you know a lot) and end up with a chapter that, at 60 or 70 pages, is far too long. Daunted by the length of your sample chapter and not sure what to do next, you might put your book aside and not return to it for some time or even indefinitely.

If you choose the second approach and make a lot or even all of the decisions about your chapter beforehand, you may create a chapter that is appropriate for your book in terms of length, structure, and content. But this approach has three significant weaknesses. First, by strictly outlining your chapter's content and length before writing it, you run the risk of imposing an inadequate or wrongheaded structure on your material. Second, focusing on strict parameters may prevent you from thinking deeply about your subject and, as a result, you may write superficially. Third, because of the constraints you've put on your chapter and on yourself, you may get bored with your writing and lose motivation to proceed.

In most circumstances a middle way is the right course. You draw the best elements from both approaches by providing yourself with enough structure to produce a manageable chapter of an appropriate length, but you allow yourself the freedom to figure out what ought to go into the chapter as you write. With this middle approach you might decide to produce a detailed outline of the chapter, which, however, you allow yourself to deviate from as you write, a rough outline that you use to remind yourself of your basic organizational ideas and any points you don't want to forget, or no outline at all.

Exercise : **WRITING YOUR SAMPLE CHAPTER**
THE MIDDLE WAY

1. Step back, look at your book as a whole, and roughly estimate how long your book ought to be. Most nonfiction books are in the range of 65,000 to 100,000 words in length, or, if you get 250 words to the page, about 260 to 400 pages in manuscript. Start with 75,000 words as a working number, which is approximately 300 pages in manuscript. Divide 300 by the number of chapters in your book to find your chapter average.

2. Ask yourself the following questions about the calculation you just arrived at:

- Does this feel like enough pages to say everything that I intend to say in this chapter?

- Does this seem like too many pages, and that I'll be stretching my material to fill the space?

In your mind's eye, lengthen or shorten your sample chapter until it feels just right. Trust your intuition that you will be able to tell when it does feel right and commit to that number as a rough guide for your sample chapter's length.

3. Lay out on the floor blank sheets of paper equal in number to the intended length of your sample chapter, to see what a chapter of this length will "look like." By visualizing your chapter in this concrete way you will gain an internal sense of how many pages you can spend on the various elements that make up your chapter and this internal sense will act as a check when you begin to write.

4. Look over your notes for the chapter and the chapter summary that you previously produced.

5. If you choose to do so, prepare a rough or detailed outline for the chapter.

6. Write your chapter, taking as many days or weeks as needed.

7. Once you've completed your sample chapter and reread it, ask yourself the question, "Am I happy with my sample chapter?" If the answer is no, revise it until it is as strong and compelling as you can make it.

8. If, after revising, you're still not happy with your sample chapter, it might be a sign that the chapter you've been working on may not be the best choice for your proposal. Repeat the process of choosing a chapter that you will use as your sample. Then write it. If it feels like a more appropriate chapter to submit, polish it until it is excellent.

Whatever approach you take to writing your sample chapter, you will end up facing the task of actually writing it. The prospect of entering this unknown territory may make you very anxious, and you may keep putting off doing it. If you find yourself balking at writing your sample chapter, try to commit to writing at least a little of it each day. If you can get to your computer and do even a little writing, your doubts and fears may lift and you will get more writing done than you had suspected you would.

STEP 2: DETERMINING THE LENGTH OF YOUR BOOK

The remaining two elements of the nonfiction book proposal are a statement of how long your book will be and how long it will take you to write it. In this section we'll look at how you can determine your book's length. Since this is something that is best done after you've written your sample chapter, now that you've done that you're in a good position to estimate your book's length.

Before you wrote your sample chapter you stepped back and looked at your book as a whole, calculated how long you thought your sample chapter ought to be, and made a tentative estimate of the length of your book based on that estimate. With the chapter written, you now have much more to go on. Let's say that you estimated that your sample chapter, one of 12 in your book, would be about 25 pages long. When you wrote the chapter you discovered that it took 30 pages to get everything that you wanted to say said. You would now raise the estimate of your book's length from 300 to 360 pages, or from 75,000 to 85,000 words. Conversely, you may have found that 20 pages were sufficient to say everything you wanted to say. Then you would reduce your estimate from 300 to 260 pages, or from 75,000 to 65,000 words.

If you find that when you multiply the length of your sample chapter by the number of chapters in your book you come up with a number quite outside the typical range, you will want to consider whether this is a good idea. If you settle on a number of words in the 65,000–100,000 range, it will strike an agent's or publisher's ear as reasonable. If, however, you decide that your book will be 40,000 words long (which may be appropriate for young adult fiction, gift books, or books of affirmations) or 140,000 words long (which might be right for historical romances, biographies, reference works, or anthologies) and your book falls into none of these categories, you may end up hurting your chances of being published.

When an agent or publisher encounters the book length figure you provide, she may recoil and lose enthusiasm for your project if it is an unusual number, either very small or very large. It is already hard enough for her to convince everyone she must convince that your book ought to be purchased without having to generate support for, say, an outsized 800-page book. Furthermore, the instant an agent or publisher is interested in your book, she will begin to think about how to price it, and price is a function of length. A publisher arrives at a cover price based in part on the length you announce in your proposal, and the price she comes up with may determine whether or not she wants to buy your book. If you say that your book will be 90,000 words long and she calculates that a book of that length must be sold at $18.95 in paperback but believes that books in your category tend to sell for $12.95, she may pass on your project. Had you said 65,000 words, you might have made the sale.

The book length you stipulate in your proposal provides information from which an agent or publisher is likely to make a variety of inferences. If you quote a very small book length in your book proposal, the reader may wonder if you really have a book there and if you have thought hard enough about what ought to be included in your book.

If you quote a large book length, she may suspect that you are too lazy or undisciplined to shape your mountain of material into a well-crafted book. Neither of these thoughts inspires her confidence. Because she is already inclined to say no—there being so many reasons to say no to any given book project—she may simply pass on your proposal. In the absence of truly excellent reasons to make your book very long or very short, staying in the normal range of 65,000–100,000 words is a good idea.

Exercise : **DETERMINING YOUR BOOK'S LENGTH**

1. Determine the length of your sample chapter in words.
2. Multiply that number by the number of chapters in your book. Add to that figure the number of words in your introduction.
3. If that total number falls within the typical range and otherwise feels right to you, that is your projected book length. If you have the intuition that your book will actually turn out to be a little shorter or a little longer than the figure you calculated, subtract or add 5,000 words and recalculate in your mind's eye if that new figure feels closer to the mark. If so, report that figure.

What if you envision that your chapters will be of varying lengths (which isn't a good idea)—how do you calculate your book's length? In that case, you will have to estimate the length of each chapter individually and add up those figures.

Remember that while the figure you announce may be only a rough approximation, it is also a real promise. Literary agents and publishers will be counting on the accuracy of that figure, within a tolerance of 5 to 10 percent, and will fully expect the manuscript you produce to be the length you quoted in your proposal. Therefore, polish your crystal ball and engage in as careful a calculation of your book's estimated length as you possibly can.

STEP 3: CALCULATING THE DELIVERY DATE

The last element of a book proposal is an announcement of when you expect to have your book completed. Agents and publishers consider this very important information. In order for a publisher to buy your book, she needs to be able to picture it in the context of the other books she publishes and know in what season your book will appear. Her company may have room for a book like yours in the spring season of the coming year but not in the fall season. Will your book be ready in time for a spring publication date, or will it need to be held back until a year from spring?

A publishing house will need from four to nine months to turn your finished manuscript into a published book, send out review copies, endorsement copies, and promotional materials, get it onto the shelves of bookstores, and so on. Nine months is more the rule than four. This means that an agent or publisher, when looking at your proposal, is adding those nine months to your statement about when your draft manuscript will be finished and predicting when your book could first appear. If that date is too far into the future—if you've said that it will take you three years to write your book—she may be inclined to skip buying it, since she can't know what her list three to four years from now ought to look like or what readers will be wanting at that time.

Generally speaking, your goal is to deliver your book sooner rather than later. So you need to set yourself a schedule that takes into account the following potential setbacks: that you can't easily find the research material that you had anticipated finding, that your book changes shape and becomes another book as you write it, that you send your editor a portion of the manuscript and she wants major changes, that life emergencies and anxieties steal your time, that you write chunks that are off target and must be discarded, that you do not write, and many others. Because every writer will face setbacks of this sort, you must take them into account when you estimate how long it will take you to complete your manuscript.

Exercise : CALCULATING HOW LONG IT WILL TAKE YOU TO COMPLETE YOUR BOOK

1. Estimate how many words you will write on each writing day. One way to gauge this is by recollecting how long it took you to write your sample chapter (but only count the days you actually did some writing on the chapter). If you aren't sure how many words you will be able to write on each writing day, use 500 words (two pages) as a rough estimate.

2. Divide the anticipated length of your book by the figure you arrived at in step 1. For example, if you anticipate that your book will be 75,000 words long and that you will write 500 words on each writing day, you would need 150 writing days to complete your manuscript.

3. Factor in setbacks and any time-consuming tasks like research and revision. You might attempt to calculate this in a detailed way, trying to gauge in your mind's eye how many days you will need to do research, how many days revising will take, how many days you will find yourself unable or unwilling to write, and so on. However, as this is virtually impossible to do with any accuracy, you might want to take the reasonable shortcut of simply doubling the figure you arrived at in step 2.

4. You may want to further protect yourself and add another two or three months to your estimate. If you've calculated that your book ought to take 10 months to write, setbacks included, you might announce that you intend to have it completed in a year. If you've calculated that it ought to take a year to write, you might say that you intend to have it finished in 15 months' time. It's far better to give yourself a few extra months than, down the road, to disappoint the editor who purchased your book or to violate the terms of your contract.

With your calculations done as to how long your book will be and when it will be completed, you are ready to write a sentence like the following: "*Elephant and Rat* will be approximately 75,000 words in length and will be available in draft 12 months after contract signing."

When you have made your calculations and written your sentence, you will have completed all of the elements of your proposal, at least in rough draft. In the next chapter we'll take a look at polishing your proposal, putting it together, and readying it for submission.

PREPARING AND SUBMITTING
YOUR PROPOSAL

n this chapter I teach you the last steps you need to take in preparing your book proposal for submission, contacting literary agents and/or publishers so as to interest them in your project, actually submitting your proposal, and handling agent and/or publisher responses to your proposal. These final steps require the same care and attention you paid to honing your concept and preparing the sections of your book proposal, as a careless misstep at the tail end of the process can harm and even ruin your chances of getting your book published.

POLISHING YOUR PROPOSAL

Once you've completed your sample chapter, chapter summaries, and the other elements of the book proposal that I've discussed so far, you will want to go back to each section and polish and improve it as the final step before submitting your proposal to agents or publishers. Not only is it likely that those sections are in rough rather than finished shape, but the recent work you did summarizing the chapters of your book and writing a sample chapter have provided you with new information that you can use to improve those earlier sections.

Exercise : POLISHING YOUR PROPOSAL

1. Bearing in mind all the work you've done to refine your book idea, prepare a one- or two-sentence description of your focused concept. The description that you prepare at this point will reflect your best current understanding of your book and will inform all aspects of your proposal as you read and revise it: how you'll focus your overview, which of your credentials you'll highlight, which books you'll compare and contrast to yours, and so on.

2. Read all of the sections of your book proposal straight through, making notes in the margins as you read. Pay special attention to any words, phrases, sentences, paragraphs, and ideas whose clarity, strength, or accuracy you doubt. When you have a doubt, put a question mark at that point.

3. Refer to the book proposal checklist on page 27. Use the questions posed there to help you determine if every section of your proposal is doing the intellectual work and the sales work that it needs to do.

4. Reread the sections of your proposal and address each of your question marks in turn. If an idea is unclear, make it clear. If a paragraph repeats the one before it, take it out. If the organizational scheme of a section feels weak, strengthen it, perhaps by re-

ordering the elements of the section, perhaps by rethinking and rewriting the section.

5. If a section is giving you trouble or doesn't feel strong, that may mean that you haven't done all the preliminary work you ought to have done. Perhaps you need to spend more hours in a bookstore and get a better idea of what books compete with and complement yours, so as to improve that section of your proposal. Maybe you need to sit down with a book like Larsen's **Guerrilla Marketing for Writers** or Kremer's **1001 Ways to Market Your Books** and garner more ideas for your marketing and promotion section. Do the legwork and thinking work it takes to make each section of your proposal shine.

PUTTING YOUR PROPOSAL TOGETHER

Once you've accomplished the work of strengthening each section of your proposal by rereading it, rethinking it, and revising it, you're ready to put the sections together into a coherent whole.

Keep the following two points in mind. Readers of your proposal, both agents and editors, are looking as much for reasons to discard your proposal as to keep reading, because they have many, many proposals to consider. Therefore, while you want to present good material throughout your proposal, you don't want to present your best material later on in your proposal, when your reader may have stopped reading already.

Second, readers of book proposals see so many proposals built exactly the same way, on models presented in one or another of the book proposal guides on the market, that varying that model in your own slightly idiosyncratic way may grab a reader's attention. Therefore, feel free to order the sections of your proposal in your own way, getting your strongest selling points and your best ideas as close to the front as you can.

Exercise: ORDERING AND PREPARING
YOUR BOOK PROPOSAL

1. Turn to the sample proposal in the appendix and note how it is organized. Remember that it is a sample and not a model, as you will want to organize your proposal in its most compelling way and not according to a formula. One typical organizational scheme is the following:

   - Title page
   - Overview
   - Testimonials (if available)
   - Format/table of contents
   - Book length and delivery date
   - Competing and complementary books
   - Marketing and promotion
   - Credentials/about the author
   - Annotated table of contents (chapter summaries)
   - Sample chapter
   - Workshop flyers or additional materials (if available)

2. If you want to see more samples before deciding on your book proposal's order, peruse Jeff Herman's book Write the Perfect Book Proposal, Larsen's book How to Write a Book Proposal, Jean Marie Stine's book Writing Successful Self-Help and How-To

Books, and/or Elizabeth Lyon's **Nonfiction Book Proposals Anybody Can Write.**

3. Your title page and overview are naturally the first two sections of your book proposal. After that, it is your choice how to put your proposal together. Play to the strengths of your project. You may feel that your competing books section does a great job of demonstrating that there is a gaping hole in the literature waiting to be filled by your book. Then put that section second, right after the overview. You may have gotten a few excellent testimonials about the importance of your ideas and feel that presenting those testimonials early on in the proposal will produce a halo effect over the sections that follow. In that case, place them right after your overview. You may be pleased with your marketing ideas and feel that they are a really strong point of your proposal. Then follow up your overview with your marketing and promotions section.

4. Determine which are the strongest elements of your proposal, the ones that would most interest a reader and best sell your project. Organize your proposal based on your understanding of the relative strengths of your various sections. Read your proposal through to see if your ordering is logical and as strong as you hoped it would be. If you have some doubts about the way you arranged the sections, try another arrangement. Reorder the elements of your proposal until you feel that you have landed on the scheme that best presents your project to a reader.

5. Put your proposal on a single computer file and format it properly: double-spaced, with pages consecutively numbered, and with adequate margins and a legible, generous-sized font. (For my book proposals I use Bookman as the font and 14 as the font size.) Your

finished book proposal will be about 20 to 80 pages in length, depending on the length of your chapter summaries and your sample chapter.

6. Print out a draft copy of your proposal and proofread it in hard copy. You will find countless small errors that you didn't catch when you read it on the computer screen, and you will also discover that you have changes to make, some small and some significant, to improve your proposal. The test of the quality of your book proposal is that it reads well in hard copy, as that is the version that literary agents and publishers will see.

7. Revise your proposal based on any changes or corrections you made when you read it in hard copy and print out a clean copy of this final version.

WRITING YOUR QUERY LETTER (OR COVER LETTER)

Once you've improved and polished every section of your proposal and put your proposal together in its strongest, most logical order, your proposal is ready to show. But you still need to create one final component: a letter to the person to whom you wish to submit the project that explains in a few clear, succinct paragraphs what your project is about and who you are.

Throughout I have used the terms *agent, publisher,* and *editor* interchangeably. Editors and publishers generally prefer to receive book proposals from agents rather than from writers who are unknown to them, so agents have the ear of editors and publishers in ways that you don't. Therefore, an agent, acting as your advocate and your intermediary, can be vitally important to you and your book project. But the fact is that agents form one group and editors and publishers form another, and you will need to decide to which group you will send your query letter and, ultimately, your proposal. In the next section I'll discuss how to decide which group to query.

Some agents and publishers prefer to have actual proposals submitted to them without any prior correspondence, in which case you would produce a cover letter that accompanies and introduces you and your project. However, most agents and publishers want you to query before submitting a proposal, in which case you would prepare an effective query letter designed to interest a reader. The only substantial difference between a query letter and a cover letter is that the cover letter, since it is accompanied by the proposal, can be even briefer than a query letter, which itself should be quite brief, no more than one and a half single-spaced pages long.

Agents and publishers tend to decide instantly whether or not a project holds some interest for them. A thumbs' up may take months as they decide how interested they actually are, but most thumbs' down take only seconds, as long as it takes to read the first sentence or two of your query letter or cover letter. Therefore, because this letter is exactly as important as writers reckon it to be, fear of writing it enters into the picture.

Out of anxiety, a writer will often spend less time on her query letter than she ought to, hoping to get it done with half an eye and half a mind. Because of fear, smoldering resentments, a stubborn refusal to play the publishing game, and other self-defeating reasons, writers regularly send lame query letters and cover letters into the world. Don't do this. Commit to writing a strong letter that is not only clear and compelling but that is better than the thousands of other query letters and cover letters that agents and publishers regularly receive.

If you write a perfunctory or, worse, confrontational query letter, you've probably doomed your chances. If you write a merely adequate query letter, one that does nothing really wrong but that doesn't stand out from the pack, you probably will not jump the high hurdle you must negotiate to interest an agent or publisher in your project. The query letter or cover letter should be your very best work.

Here are two examples of strong query letters:

[Your letterhead]

[Date]

Dear Mary Jane Agent:

Over the course of a successful decade-long acting career I've discovered that the biggest concern actors have is figuring out what skills will help them survive in our fiercely competitive industry. Realizing that there is no basic book that helps them identify these necessary skills, I began interviewing working actors and asking them to spell out what had helped them succeed. These interviews and the further research I did led me to identify 12 business survival skills that every working actor needs to master.

Many books have been written about the craft of acting and the lives of actors. But you need more than classes in improv and sword-fighting and a set of head shots to succeed as a working actor. You need the resourcefulness of a rat, the adaptability of a chameleon, the independence of a cat, the armor of an elephant, and much more. *Elephant and Rat* is the first book to offer concrete, direct-from-the-trenches advice on how to acquire the 12 survival skills every actor must master.

While actors make up a relatively small market, they are dedicated buyers and readers of any book that will give them an edge.

Self-help and how-to books that prepare them for auditions, like Ed Hooks's *The Audition Book,* or that demystify the business, like Marilyn Henry's *How to Be a Working Actor* (going strong after 15 years), are constant sellers that go into multiple printings. In addition, actors can be reached through book clubs like Stage and Screen Book Club, trade publishers like Back Stage Books and Drama Publishers, and online affinity groups like Acting-Pro, Perform, and Stagecraft.

I hope you'll be interested in looking at my proposal, which is complete at this time. An envelope is enclosed for your reply.

Sincerely

John Q. Writer

Here's a second example:

[Your letterhead]

[Date]

Dear Mary Jane Agent:

Much of the time that we grew up together, I hated my younger sister. I lived in the shadow of her vitality and struggled to define myself against her. By her late twenties she'd earned her law degree and at 35 she took over my father's law practice—but then, at 38, she was diagnosed with a fatal brain tumor. Suddenly I became responsible for taking care of a sister whom I loved, hated, and feared through her agonizing and prolonged death.

I am writing a memoir about these experiences called *A Blossom in the Brain.* I bring both writing skills and psychological insight to this project. With Master's degrees in Creative Writing and Social Work, I've taught memoir writing at the University of

Minnesota and I give lectures frequently nationally and internationally.

A Blossom in the Brain examines the love-hate relationship between two sisters. This memoir of blood rivals facing their bitter
differences as one ministers to the dying of the other is a special
story. Please let me know if you would like to see the complete
book proposal for this memoir.

Sincerely,

Jane Q. Writer

The query letter seems like a simple document to write, but the
truth is, it's very hard to speak brilliantly about a book project, even
one that you know as well as you know your own. It is very hard to pin
down an idea and present it so that another person is intrigued by it—
or even interested in it. The task of writing a strong query letter is
simple in the abstract but difficult in reality. The following steps will
take you through the process of creating a strong query letter. Just be
forewarned—it may take you longer to create this short document
than to write your entire sample chapter. However, it will be well
worth it to spend all the time you need, as your diligent work can help
your query letter stand out from the pack.

Exercise : CREATING YOUR QUERY LETTER

1. Reread your book proposal, especially your overview and credentials sections, and extract the best ideas and the strongest selling
   points to include in your query letter. Write down a list of these
   ideas: for example, that you've had a successful acting career, that
   you've conducted interviews with actors, that you've learned ex-

actly what it takes to survive in the acting business, that you've culled what you've learned into 12 clear principles, and so on.

2. Write a one-page, single-spaced first draft of your query letter and reread it carefully, looking for any words, phrases, sentences, or ideas that feel second best. Operate on the principle that less is more. Take out any unclear ideas, lazy phrases, or hint of a negative attitude. Focus not on your needs but on the needs of the person reading the letter, who requires a clear presentation of your major points and reasons to like your project.

3. Rewrite your query letter as many times as necessary until it is tight and excellent. Do not settle for anything less than excellence. At the end of the process you should have a one-page, single-spaced document that is clear, interesting, compelling, and easy to read.

4. If you don't already have some, purchase letterhead stationery or prepare some using your computer's software design capabilities. The information you want your letterhead to include are your name, mailing address, phone number, fax number, and e-mail address. You don't need to call yourself "Writer" or "Freelance Writer" or anything of that sort, though of course if you have a professional designation you would include that information.

5. Print out a draft copy of your letter on your letterhead.

6. Read your draft letter in hard copy. Ask yourself, "If I received this letter out of the blue, would I be interested in this book and this author?" If the answer to either part is no, revise and strengthen your query letter until you can answer yes to both parts.

7. As an optional step, show your draft letter to one or more friends. Use their feedback to strengthen your letter.

DECIDING WHERE TO SEND YOUR PROPOSAL

Now that you have your book proposal and your query letter completed, your next task is deciding where you will be sending it. The first decision you must make is whether you will approach literary agents, book editors, or both groups simultaneously. My advice is that in general you should seek representation by a literary agent first, rather than trying to approach publishers. Many, if not most, large publishing houses won't consider your query letter or your book proposal and prefer to deal exclusively with literary agents. Therefore, garnering the services of a literary agent is vital.

However, there are exceptions to this general rule. If you've had personal contact with a book editor at a writers' conference and she expressed interest in your work, then you might query her directly, reminding her of the conversation the two of you had. And if you are not necessarily looking for a large publishing house, there are only a few small to middle-sized publishers who might be interested in your book (because of its specialized nature, say), and you can identify those publishers, you may want to query them directly.

If you decide to approach literary agents with your query letter, you will need to know which ones to contact. One common-sense approach is to consider recommendations from writers and editors given at writers' conferences or in published interviews. There are also several books on the market that will introduce you to literary agents, explain how they operate, and help you decide which ones to query. These include Herman's *Writer's Guide to Book Editors, Publishers, and Literary Agents,* Larsen's *Literary Agents: What They Do, How They Do It, and How to Find and Work with the Right One for You,* Donya Dickerson's *Guide to Literary Agents: 570 Agents Who Sell What You Write,* Debby

Meyer's *Literary Agents: The Essential Guide for Writers,* and John Baker's *Literary Agents: A Writer's Introduction.*

Gather information on literary agents, learning as best you can which ones handle projects like yours. One way to do this is by looking at the acknowledgments pages of books like yours that you admire. Use your research to help you generate a list of possible agents. You will then need to decide whether you will approach them one at a time or engage in "multiple submissions." In general, I would suggest that you send out your query letter in multiple submission, meaning that you would send it out to several agents simultaneously. Always indicate this fact in your letter, perhaps in a postscript in which you say, "Please note that I am querying a few agents simultaneously."

An exception to the rule of querying several agents at once would be if a particular literary agent has previously expressed interest in your work. If you have decided to approach this agent, you should query him or her and wait for a response before querying other agents, giving that agent an exclusive chance to represent your project. You would indicate this fact in your query letter with a line such as "You have this exclusively."

Exercise : **DECIDING WHERE TO SEND YOUR PROPOSAL**

1. Determine whether you will query agents or editors. Is your book going to a small house? Do you know any editors? If not, you should focus on sending to agents.
2. Learn from directories and other sources which literary agents or niche publishers you will contact.

3. If you are going to contact publishers, call each publishing house and find out who the right person would be to query. Also ask for a catalog. Publishers' catalogs are full of useful information about current and past titles and will give you the best idea of what kinds of books each house publishes.

4. Prepare your list of likely agents or likely publishers. Your list of agents ought to be on the long side rather than the short side (twelve, say, rather than two), since querying many agents increases your odds of eventually landing representation. However, the length of your list of publishers will depend on how many houses you locate that publish books like yours, and may include only two or three likely candidates.

PREPARING YOURSELF FOR THE SUBMISSION PROCESS

Before you send out even your first query letter, you will want to prepare yourself practically and psychologically for the possibility that a literary agent or an editor may eventually contact you by telephone to get answers to questions that are on her mind. When a reader of your query letter is interested in your project but still has some doubts about whether she wants to see your complete proposal, she is quite likely to pick up the telephone and give you a call. You should be ready for this call.

Agents or editors may want to talk to you about a range of things, from your concept to your marketing plans, or they may just want to get a sense of who you are and how professional you seem. Because it's unlikely that you're currently prepared to answer the questions that agents or editors may toss at you, I've come up with a list of the 20 most common questions that you might be asked. The following exercise will help you deliver your responses to these 20 questions with confidence and clarity. Prepare your answers and memorize them—or, at worst, have them sitting by your telephone—so that you will be prepared to handle those rare but important phone calls that can come out of the blue from literary agents and publishers.

Exercise : PREPARING 20 ANSWERS

Prepare strong answers to the following 20 questions. Keep the answers brief, so that you can remember them and so that you stay focused in this "interview" situation and not cause your caller to lose interest. If you are printing them out to keep by your phone, print them out in a very large font size so that you can read them even if you are feeling anxious.

Here are the 20 most common questions an agent or editor is likely to ask you:

1. What's your book about?
2. Where in the bookstore do you see your book being shelved?
3. What makes your book special?
4. What about it will interest readers the most?
5. What are the two or three things that separate your book from other books like it?
6. Why is it a good book for the current market?
7. Who do you see as your target audience?
8. What books are like yours?
9. What do you see as some ways to reach your intended audience?
10. What will you do to help sell your book?
11. What have you written before?
12. Why do you think you're the right person to write this book?

13. How much of your manuscript is done?

14. When would you have it completed?

15. How long will it be?

16. From an agent: What publishing houses do you see as possibly wanting to publish it? From a publisher: Why do you think our house is the right house for this book?

17. Do you have any special connections that will help the book sell?

18. Do you like to do or do you have any experience with public speaking?

19. Are you planning to create workshops or give lectures based on your book?

20. What other books do you have in mind to write?

In addition to preparing the text of your answers to common agent or editor questions, you will want to prepare yourself emotionally for what most writers consider to be a highly stressful situation. Every time you interact with an agent or a publisher you will be communicating a wealth of information about your personality and your attitude, and thereby either doing yourself some good or some harm. How do you want to present yourself? In a word, professionally. You want to be polite, agreeable, friendly, focused, and flexible. You want to listen carefully and speak just as carefully. However, this is far easier to say than it is for the average writer to manage.

When you're communicating with agents and editors you're likely to feel anxious, maybe a little angry (that the agent seems so rushed or that the editor has forgotten the title of your book), maybe a little desperate (because you know that if you say the wrong thing you may have ruined your chances with this agent or editor), maybe a little aggressive (because you dislike people who hold so much power over you), and so on. Recognize your own feelings and keep in the front of your mind that your job is to act professionally, to clearly hear what is being said and to say what is in your best interests to say, to not sabotage yourself, and to not burn bridges. Remember the following 12 rules for talking with agents and publishers:

1. Leave out any hint of self-disparagement.
   Wrong: "I haven't been writing all that long."
   Right: "I've been writing for more than five years."
2. Act like you know what your book is about.
   Wrong: "I think my book may be about . . ."
   Right: "My book is about . . ."
3. Act like you are the right person to write your book.
   Wrong: "I know that someone with more experience might treat the subject differently . . ."
   Right: "I am passionate about my subject and I'm the right person to write this book."
4. Display lots of ego strength but no ego.
   Wrong: "I think I have makings of a great writer, if only somebody will give me a chance . . ."
   Right: "This book will be very strong."
5. Be clear and direct.
   Wrong: "I've had the opportunity to connect with the forensic details in my book over the past dozen years both in a lab setting and in the field . . ."
   Right: "I've been a coroner for 12 years."
6. Be precise.
   Wrong: "My book will be about average length."
   Right: "My book will be 70,000 words in length."

7. Don't make any subtle accusations.

Wrong: "Now you won't let my proposal get lost in your piles of submissions, will you?"

Right: "I look forward to hearing from you and working with you."

8. Stay on track.

Wrong: "I had the funniest thing happen to me earlier today . . ."

Right: "Another one of my book's strengths is . . ."

9. Be positive.

Wrong: "I know there are lots of books on this subject in the bookstores . . ."

Right: "Readers are always looking for another good book on this subject . . ."

10. Ask only *relevant* questions.

Wrong: "How many books will you publish next year?"

Right: "I think I just heard you say that you're a little worried about my target audience. Would you like more clarification on that point?"

11. Stay positive after each body blow.

Wrong: "Oh, so you think my idea is stupid!"

Right: "Is there a better way I might work with my idea? Do you have any suggestions?"

12. Don't burn bridges.

Wrong: "Well, I guess *we* won't ever be working together."

Right: "Thank you."

Exercise : **TAKING CALLS OUT OF THE BLUE**

1. Have a friend call you out of the blue and pretend to be an agent or editor who wants to chat with you about your book. Prepare her so that she can ask you some or all of the 20 questions I named earlier.

2. After the conversation, ask your friend for feedback on the quality of your responses and on how you deported yourself. Use her observations and suggestions to help you determine what you might do to improve your performance.

SENDING OUT YOUR QUERY LETTER
OR BOOK PROPOSAL

Earlier you prepared your list of names and addresses of agents and/or publishers to whom you will be sending your query letter or your book proposal. Print out your query letter for each agent or publisher you intend to query, and print out your cover letter and photocopy a clean copy of your book proposal for each agent or publisher to whom you are sending the complete proposal.

Send out each query letter in a plain envelope and each proposal package in a reinforced (bubble) mailer, enclosing a stamped, self-addressed envelope for reply with each. As it is better not to recycle proposals, since they get battered and shopworn, there is no need to enclose a bubble mailer for the return of your proposal. Simply mention in your cover letter that the reader should discard the proposal if it is not of interest to him or her.

It's a good idea to keep track of your submissions in a notebook or on your computer. I use a notebook and I also keep in my office a large erasable board on which I note who is currently looking at my query letters or book proposals (for projects not being represented by my literary agent). While it may seem like a duplication to keep a notebook and repeat the information on an erasable board, I find it very helpful to keep track of my proposals' progress in both ways, in recorded form in a book and in a visible way on a big board that I encounter frequently.

AFTER THE SUBMISSIONS HAVE GONE OUT

Once you begin to submit your query letter or book proposal to agents or publishers, you will begin to receive responses. There are several possible responses you can expect:

- You may hear from an agent or publisher who has questions and is looking for clarification.
- You may receive a form rejection letter or a personalized rejection letter.
- You may hear from an agent or publisher who is interested in your proposal but who indicates that he or she will only represent or publish your book if you make certain changes.
- You may receive an invitation to submit your book proposal to an agent or a publisher in response to your query.
- You may receive an offer of representation from an agent.
- You may receive an offer from a publisher to publish your book.
- You may receive no response, which is also a kind of response.

Let's consider the last first and the remainder in order.

If you do not hear from an agent or a publisher for a considerable length of time—say, six to eight weeks—you might recontact him or her with a short letter or a postcard, indicating your hope that your initial query letter or proposal arrived safely. With agents, you might conceivably call rather than write, but you are likely to do yourself more harm than good with this approach. After all, the agent hasn't looked at your query letter or proposal yet, or has looked at it but isn't interested, or has looked at it, finds it of some interest, and is mulling over how interested she really is. Your phone call out of the blue does you no good in the first two scenarios and does you only some possible good in the third, but only if you do an excellent (and speedy) job of presenting your project. On balance, it is better to check in with a brief note; if you still don't hear after a few more months have elapsed, scratch that agent or publisher from your list.

We've already discussed how you should prepare yourself in case you hear from an agent or a publisher who is looking for clarification. The main point to remember is that you want to come across as professional, flexible, and helpful when an agent or publisher calls to discuss your project. Make sure that you get the person's name, his or her literary agency or publishing house, and, if possible, a phone number where he or she can be reached. As soon as the conversation ends, evaluate your performance. It's likely that you will feel that you didn't do as good a job as you wanted, either in presenting your project or yourself or in answering the caller's questions. In that case, prepare and rehearse your "better" responses and give the person a call. Do not feel shy about doing this, as the agent's or publisher's phone call and expression of interest entitles you to at least one return call.

When you receive a form rejection letter, make a note of that fact in your submission log and remove that person from your erasable board. There is no real information to be gleaned from the language of a form rejection and you don't want to leap from some innocent phrase—for instance, "We feel that it would be difficult to place your work in today's market"—to some conclusion about your book's merits or marketplace potential. Unless an agent or publisher makes specific comments about your project, pay no attention to the language of the rejection letter.

If you receive a personalized rejection, send that person a thank-you note. If, in the personalized rejection, the agent or publisher asks you to keep her in mind for future projects, put her name on a special list that you keep of persons to approach with a new project or with a revised version of this project. If she offers you some advice about your book idea or your proposal, consider that advice carefully. But remember that she is rejecting your proposal, so the advice she is offering may be a little on the idle side.

It is quite a different matter when an agent or editor expresses an interest in your work and has suggestions about changes he or she thinks you ought to make. In this case, you will want to seriously consider whether you think the changes are appropriate and wise to make. Remember that a reader who suggests changes, even though he may be interested in your project, is not guaranteeing that he will represent your book or publish it should you make the changes. He is only saying that if you make the changes he will probably look at the new proposal to see if it interests him.

When and if an agent or publisher expresses interest in seeing your proposal, you might, as a courtesy and a matter of strategy, extend that individual an exclusive look. However, find out how long the agent or publisher thinks it will take her to make a decision, as your proposal will be unproductively tied up for that length of time if she ultimately passes on the project. Once an agent or a publisher is exclusively considering your project, you would reply to any other agents or publishers who contact you and express interest in your proposal that you would be happy to show them the proposal when it becomes available again.

If an agent asks to represent your project, thank him and ask to have a copy of his agency contract faxed to you, along with a list of the books he has recently sold. When you have the contract and book list in hand, take a day to look them over, reflect on your phone conversation with him, discuss the agent with published writer friends or other publishing insiders you know, and, if you're in the mind to do so, investigate him on the Internet at writers' sites where agents are discussed.

If he wants to charge a fee to represent you, as opposed to taking a commission from sales (usually 15 percent), you may want to pass, as fee-charging is frowned on by most reputable agents. Similarly, if he recommends that you avail yourself of a particular editorial service because your proposal needs improving, or in any way suggests that you part with a significant amount of money, beware. There are some unscrupulous agents out there who prey on writers and who make most of their money from the writers they fleece, not from selling writers' books to publishers.

You should also take notice of whether you are contracting for representation of this proposal alone or for all your current and future projects. Each agent has a preferred way of operating, and the language of his or her contract will spell this out. You retain more freedom if the agent is only representing this particular project, but you may get a greater level of commitment from an agent who is contracting to represent all of your projects. Often an agent will agree to change the language of the contract if you have a preference, especially if your preference is that he only represent your current project.

When you've made your decision, contact the agent and let him know what you've decided. Since representation is very hard to acquire, even if you have some doubts about the agent's personality or track record you might still incline toward saying yes. However, if you have a strong intuitive hunch or some telling evidence that it might be best not to work with this agent, then politely pass. Once you agree to agency representation, contact the other agents who are looking at your query letter or proposal and let them know that you have chosen agency representation. In a brief letter, thank them for the time they've spent considering your query or proposal.

This covers all possible responses but one.

IF YOU GET AN OFFER

If you have submitted your proposal to a publisher and you receive a telephone offer to publish your book, make notes as you converse with the editor or publisher regarding any important points she brings up: the advance she is offering, whether the book will be a paperback or a hardback, how long she thinks the book ought to be, when she needs the manuscript delivered by, and any other significant matters that may come up in this initial conversation. Genuinely thank her for her interest but make sure not to agree at this time to the amount of the advance she is offering or to any other details of the deal. Rather, inform her that you will get back to her in a day or two with your thoughts.

In order to help you make up your mind whether to accept or reject her offer to publish your book and whether or not to counter the amount of the advance she is offering, ask your published writer friends or other marketplace insiders their opinion of this house and this offer, familiarize yourself with one or more of the books on the market that walk writers through the process of negotiating a book contract, and, if you like, call a literary agent or two to discuss the publishing house and the offer. An agent may be willing to chat with you for free and/or look at the contract for an hourly fee.

Books that you might consult include Mark Levine's *Negotiating a Book Contract,* Jonathan Kirsch's *Kirsch's Guide to the Book Contract,* Ted Crawford's book *The Writer's Legal Guide,* Brad Bunnin's *The Writer's Legal Companion,* and Richard Curtis's *How to Be Your Own Literary Agent.* Additionally, both the National Writers Union and the Literary Guild publish information on understanding and negotiating book contracts.

If you accept the publisher's offer, let any other parties who might be considering your proposal know that you are withdrawing your proposal from consideration. In a brief letter, thank them for the time they've spent considering your query letter or proposal. Then uncork a bottle of champagne and celebrate.

WRITING YOUR NONFICTION BOOK
NOW OR LATER

The process I've described for arriving at a focused book idea and preparing a compelling book proposal is at least as arduous—and can take as long—as writing the book itself. It is not unusual to spend a year wrestling your idea and your proposal into existence and then less than a year writing your book once a publisher has expressed the desire to publish it. If you've arrived at the point of submitting your proposal to agents or publishers, you've gone a long way toward creating your nonfiction book, maybe as much as half of the way.

In the best-case scenario, the following will happen. An agent will agree to represent your book. Your book will be sold to a publisher, who will be happy with the format and content of your book as you described them in your book proposal. Your table of contents will serve as the template for your book as you write it. Your chapter summaries will keep you focused like a laser on the central intention of each chapter. You will keep to the schedule you calculated when you determined how long it would take you to write your book, and you will write a draft of your book by the date announced in your book contract.

Right now, however, while you're as yet "unattached" to a publisher, you have two basic choices. You can write your proposed book while you attempt to sell it, or you can start to work on a completely different project. The up side of beginning to write your original book now is that you'll be that much closer to completing it if an offer to publish it arrives. However, because that offer may entail your changing your book to suit the vision of the publisher, you might decide to wait to write your book until you and a publisher have agreed on its shape and content. This will leave you free to begin to create a second book (and a second book proposal) at this time.

If you decide to go this route, your initial task is to arrive at a second focused book idea and to do the same kind of systematic, careful thinking that you engaged in with your first book idea. Your new idea, when you find it, will either be related or unrelated to your original idea. If it is related to your original idea, consider carefully whether this is the right moment to embark on a book proposal similar to the one that you are currently circulating. It may be wiser to embark on a book that is quite different from your first. Because it covers new ground, a completely new book is likely to feel fresher and more interesting to you.

Whether your new book idea is similar to or different from your original idea, you will want to proceed just as you did with your first book proposal, following the steps I've previously outlined. Forgo tinkering with the proposal that is currently circulating and focus your energies on crafting excellent sections of your new proposal.

While it may not be any easier to bring your second book proposal into being than your first, you will have learned a lot from that prior experience and you have every likelihood of making use of those important lessons with your new project.

Whichever path you choose—whether you embark on the exciting journey of writing your book or the equally adventurous journey of creating another nonfiction book proposal—congratulate yourself on having come this far. Many people dream of writing a nonfiction book, but few translate their vague ideas into a focused book idea or create a compelling book proposal. If you are one of these few, I wish you the best of luck in selling your nonfiction proposal and ultimately writing a meaningful, successful book.

SAMPLE BOOK PROPOSAL

The majority of nonfiction book proposals that writers send out to literary agents and publishers are sent out either in poor shape or at best in fair shape. Few are in excellent shape. So few are in excellent shape that neither my editor, who sees hundreds upon hundreds of proposals, nor I could see our way to including an actual proposal we've encountered as a model of what a nonfiction book proposal should contain. But we nevertheless felt that you should see at least one complete proposal, so we decided to include one of my own, not because it is perfect but rather because with it you can least see all the parts of a book proposal in clear working order.

The proposal I'm choosing to show you is for a book called *The Van Gogh Blues: The Creative Person's Path Through Depression.* This proposal has a pair of virtues as a teaching example. First, as the two publishers to see it each made an offer to publish it, I believe it is an example of an effective book proposal. Second, it announces a book with a limited appeal. While publishers hope that every book they publish will have commercial success, they nevertheless have different expectations for each title. They have high hopes for a few titles, because of the author's track record, the timeliness or wide appeal of the subject, or some similar consideration, and they cross their fingers about the rest. *The Van Gogh Blues* is one of the "rest." Few editors would expect a book about creative people managing their depression to become a bestseller. Therefore, it has a built-in hurdle to overcome: it must appeal for reasons other than that it has bestseller written all over it. The fact that it negotiated this hurdle should make it of interest to you.

The proposal as you find it here is somewhat different from the proposal I originally submitted and includes some changes that were made after the book was purchased by its publisher. As the proposal is annotated, you will get to see what those changes were and why I made them. I hope that the annotations help you better understand how to build and order your own book proposal. Remember that this is an example, not a model, and that you will want to put your book proposal together in the way that allows you to present your case in its most compelling fashion.

[LETTERHEAD]

June 15, 2001

Dear Ms. Agent:[1]

Over the course of my 20 years counseling and coaching writers, artists, musicians, and other creative individuals, I've learned that the most significant emotional problem they face is depression. I've also learned that biological remedies like antidepressants and psychological remedies like psychotherapy have only a limited ability to treat this depression, because it is existential in nature. In *The Van Gogh Blues: The Creative Person's Path Through Depression,* I spell out the reasons for this epidemic of depression among creative people and provide 10 strategies creators can immediately put to use to prevent and combat their depression.

I've written more than 20 books, a dozen of them in the creativity field. Among these are seven with Tarcher/Penguin (including *Fearless Creating, Deep Writing,* and *The Creativity Book*) and books with Harper San Francisco, Adams Media, New World Library, and other mainstream houses. My creativity books have sold between 150,000 and 200,000 copies and I have many thousands of loyal readers who look forward to each of my new books. I have done national media, including CNBC, NBC News, Fox News, *Thinking Allowed,* and *To Tell the Truth,* scores of radio and print interviews, and hundreds of book sign-

---

[1] I've prepared this query letter for the sake of this appendix. In actual fact, I never prepared a query letter for this project. Rather, I had a phone conversation with my agent in which I described the project and asked him if he wanted to see it. He did, chose to represent it, and subsequently sold it.

ings, conference appearances, lectures, and workshops. In 2001, I was the keynote speaker at the Jack London Writers Conference, and in 2002, I was one of five core faculty members of the Paris Writers Workshop.

The Van Gogh Blues is the first book to explain why creators get depressed and to provide them with real help for their depression. I hope you will be interested in looking at the proposal for *The Van Gogh Blues,* which is complete at this time. An envelope is enclosed for your reply.

Sincerely,

Eric Maisel, Ph.D.

P.S. I am querying a few agents simultaneously on this project.

THE VAN GOGH BLUES:
THE CREATIVE PERSON'S
PATH THROUGH DEPRESSION[2]

• • *proposal* • •

Eric Maisel, Ph.D.
ericmaisel@hotmail.com[3]
415-824-2113

"Maisel has made a career out of helping artists
and writers cope with the traumas and troubles
that are the price of admission to a creative life."[4]
—Intuition Magazine

---

[2] In the proposal as submitted, the subtitle I used was "a guide to understanding and treating creators' depression." But I subsequently came to feel that this subtitle made psychotherapists seem like the book's primary intended readership, which was too narrow and not accurate in any case.

[3] In my experience, if a literary agent or editor is interested enough in a proposal even to ask a question, she will e-mail or call rather than write. So, while my mailing address appears on my stationery, I don't include it on a proposal's title page.

[4] You may feel self-conscious about touting yourself, but it is far better to make a case for yourself than, out of embarrassment and awkwardness, to hide your accomplishments under a barrel.

THE VAN GOGH BLUES:
THE CREATIVE PERSON'S
PATH THROUGH DEPRESSION

Overview[5]

Creative people often battle depression their whole lives.[6] When they seek relief, they are generally told that either their depression is biological and must be treated with antidepressants or it is psychological and therapy is the answer. They are never told that their depression is existential, that they are upset about the facts of existence, and that unless they restore meaning to their lives they will continue to suffer. *The Van Gogh Blues* is the first book[7] to describe the special depression that creators experience and to offer solutions that creators can immediately put into practice.

It has been known for thousands of years, since Aristotle wrote about the emotional problems of creators, that creative individuals suffer from depression and other mood disorders like mania at really alarming rates. But the reasons for this epidemic of depression have never been adequately explored, and no one has come forward with a sensible treatment plan. I[8] am a creativity expert with twenty years of

---

[5] This proposal was submitted to publishers by my agent and so I didn't write a query letter for it. Had I needed to write one, I would have used this first paragraph and a single paragraph about my credentials, leading with my credentials.

[6] This simple sentence does a lot of work. The primary work it does is announce that a large market exists for the book, namely virtually all creative people.

[7] If your book is not the first book to do something, then of course you wouldn't say it was. But if you believe that it is, you will want to announce that at the very beginning of your proposal.

[8] You have the choice whether to write in the first person or the third person. Of the 16 examples of successful proposals in Larsen's *How to Write a Book Proposal* and Herman's *Write the Perfect Book Proposal*, 15 are written in the third person. Elizabeth Lyon, in *Nonfiction Book Proposals Anybody Can*

experience as a therapist and creativity coach, and in *The Van Gogh Blues* I present a comprehensive treatment plan that any writer, painter, musician, scientist, inventor, or other creative person can immediately put into practice. For the first time the existential nature of creators' depression is explained and treatment options are spelled out.

The Van Gogh Blues is informed by my interactions with the two thousand readers of my monthly creativity newsletter,[9] who have responded enthusiastically to my explanation of creators' depression. Based on my clinical and coaching experience, my work as a trainer of creativity coaches, my understanding of the creativity and depression literature, and my involvement with creative people in a variety of settings, *The Van Gogh Blues* provides creative and would-be creative people with the help they need in dealing with their inevitable depression.

Early Endorsements

Several experts in the depression field have already expressed their enthusiasm for *The Van Gogh Blues*. Here is one early endorsement:

"Maisel's concepts in *The Van Gogh Blues* are right on the mark and address an area that is critically important and that has been largely neglected. In addition, his writing style is superb. I also appreciated that he mentioned the role of medical treatment in some forms of depression. People who espouse a particular position often narrowly focus on that one area, but Maisel has done a great job maintaining a

---

Write, explained: "Speaking about yourself from the narrator's position lets you tout your qualifications without sounding like an egomaniac." If you are proposing a book like a memoir you might opt for a first-person presentation, but third person is the standard practice, and for good reasons. I have used the third person in the "about the author" section and the first person in the other sections of the proposal, to show you how each sounds.

[9] You will have to decide when a number is "impressive enough" to mention. I think that having two thousand subscribers to my newsletter will come across as a positive. However, later on in the proposal I make the decision to leave certain numbers out, as they are not impressive enough.

broad perspective. His ideas are important ones and they have gotten me thinking."[10]

—John Preston, author of *Depression and Anxiety Management* and *A Consumer's Guide to Psychiatric Drugs*

I plan to solicit other endorsements from well-known authors and experts in the depression/creativity fields, among them Kay Jamison, author of the bestselling *Touched with Fire: Manic-Depressive Illness and the Artistic Temperament*; Linda Leonard, author of *Witness to the Fire: Creativity and the Veil of Addiction*; Jablow Hershman, author of *Manic Depression and Creativity*; and Albert Lubin, author of *Stranger on the Earth: A Psychological Biography of Vincent van Gogh.*

Length and Delivery Date

The Van Gogh Blues will be approximately 75,000 words in length[11] and will be completed eight months after contract signing.[12] The introduction and an annotated table of contents are included with this proposal.[13]

---

[10] I could have included other, quite excellent, endorsements, but it seemed to me that this was a case of less being more. I didn't want to tax my reader's patience with too many endorsements.

[11] At this point I had produced a 5,000-word introduction and a 10,000-word appendix. The book was to have 12 chapters, and I recokoned that each of them would be about 5,000 words in length.

[12] When the book was purchased, the publisher wondered If I could produce the book in five months, rather than eight, as a spot for the book was available on the publisher's spring 2002 list. Although I was worried about whether I could produce the book that quickly, I agreed, thinking that I would simply do the best I could to meet that shortened deadline.

[13] I didn't think it necessary to say anything more about the book's format, as I felt that the introduction and annotated table of contents would speak for themselves. I therefore included my entire "format section" as part of the "length and delivery" section. If I had wanted to alert my reader to the fact that the book might have illustrations, as I hoped it would, I would have written up a separate format section. But I meant to hold the discussion about possible illustrations in abeyance until the book was sold to a publisher, as I have found that any mention of illustrations is a "potential objection" that can get in the way of making a sale.

Competing and Complementary Books

Only a handful of books have looked at the relationship between creativity and depression. All of these fall into two camps, those that presume that depression is biological and those that presume that it is psychological. The best-known book is one from the first camp, Kay Jamison's *Touched with Fire: Manic-Depressive Illness and the Artistic Temperament* (Free Press, 1993, paper), in which she argues that a wide variety of creative figures have had the "hereditary disease" of bipolar disorder (manic-depression). She supports her argument by providing lists of depressed creative people and presenting clinical descriptions of famous artists. Her only advice for the creative person is to take antidepressants, and she offers no rationale for the connection between creativity and depression.

A similar book is Jablow Hershman's *Manic Depression and Creativity* (Prometheus Books, 1998, paper), which also looks at a handful of historical figures, Newton, Beethoven, and Dickens among them. Hershman argues that these figures were all manic-depressive but offers no explanations as to why this might be so and presents no advice for the creative person suffering from depression. Other books in this vein include Thomas Caramagno's *The Flight of the Mind: Virginia Woolf's Art and Manic-Depressive Illness* (University of California Press, 1992, paper) and Arnold Ludwig's *The Price of Greatness: Resolving the Creativity and Madness Controversy* (Guilford Press, 1995, paper).

Many books have been written that examine some aspect of creativity and depression from a psychological point of view or that look at a single creator's depression through the lens of psychology. These include books like Albert Lubin's *Stranger on the Earth: A Psychological Biography of Vincent van Gogh* (Holt, 1972, paper), Alice Miller's

The Untouched Key: Tracing Childhood Trauma in Creativity and Destructiveness (Doubleday, 1990, paper), and John Gedo's *Portraits of the Artist* (Analytic Press, 1989, paper). These books, most of which argue from discredited psychoanalytic theory, have nothing to offer a creative person looking for help or hoping to understand her own depression.

There have also been a few first-person accounts, most notably William Styron's bestselling *Darkness Visible: A Memoir of Madness* (Random House, 1990) and Kay Jamison's bestselling memoir of her manic-depressive illness. But no book has appeared that sets out to explain the relationship between creativity and depression and that sets as its goal *helping* creative people deal with depression. So far, all books in this genre have been descriptive and have been limited even in that regard by their reliance on unsupported biological and psychological theory. *The Van Gogh Blues* leaps ahead by presenting a new picture of creators' depression and by offering prescriptions, not descriptions.

Of the books that do offer help for creative people, like Julia Cameron's bestselling *The Artist's Way* (Tarcher/Putnam, 1992), Natalie Goldberg's bestselling *Writing Down the Bones* (Shambhala, 1986), Jan Phillips's *Marry Your Muse* (Quest Books, 1997), Victoria Nelson's *On Writer's Block* (Houghton Mifflin, 1993), Sally Warner's *Making Room for Making Art* (Chicago Review Press, 1994), Bonnie Friedman's *Writing Past Dark* (Harper, 1993), and many others in this category, none were written by a trained psychotherapist or designed to provide help with the depression creators experience.[14]

---

[14] This section is divided into four thematic groups: biological books, psychological books, first-person accounts, and self-help books for creative people. I left out any mention of general books on depression, which might have made for a fifth grouping, as including that, it seemed to me, would have lessened the overall effectiveness of this section.

About the Author

Eric Maisel, Ph.D., is an internationally known creativity expert, creativity coach, psychotherapist, and bestselling author whose creativity books have sold well in excess of 150,000 copies. In 2000, two new books by Maisel appeared: *The Creativity Book* (Tarcher) and *Twenty Communication Tips For Families* (New World Library). In 2001, *Sleep Thinking* (Adams Media) and *Twenty Communication Tips At Work* (New World Library) debuted. In 2002, *Write Mind* (Tarcher) will appear, and in 2004, *The Art of the Book Proposal* (Tarcher) will be published.[15]

Maisel's books in the creativity field include *Fearless Creating,*[16] *A Life in the Arts, Affirmations for Artists, Artists Speak, Deep Writing, Fearless Presenting, The Creativity Book,* and *Living the Writer's Life.* Maisel founded and wrote *Callboard Magazine's* "Staying Sane in the Theater" column and regularly presents on creativity issues, for example at the 1998 and 1999 Romance Writers of America conference, the 1999 American Psychological Association conference, the Aspen and Santa Fe Creativity and Madness conferences, the Pacific Voice Conference, annual conferences of the California Association of Marriage and Family Therapists and the California Career Development Association, and many others. His articles have appeared in *Intuition Magazine, Writer's Digest, Dramatics Magazine,* and *The California Therapist,* among others.

Maisel's books have been the choice of many book clubs, among them

---

[15] Generally, agents and editors are not happy to see so many titles appear from one author, especially when they involve different publishing houses. It raises the suspicion that the author is spreading himself too thin and can't possibly promote each of his books adequately, that perhaps he is "jumping" from publisher to publisher because of difficulties he creates, and so on. But of course it is also impressive to have so many books appear. Since there isn't really any way to avoid reporting the facts of the matter, I try to state them simply, without embarrassment and without trying to "defend" the fact that six of my books will appear in a four-year span.

[16] It might seem sensible and useful to mention the number of copies sold of each of my books, but in my experience the numbers, being modest, strike an agent or publisher's ear more as a negative than a positive. Therefore I only mention the aggregate number, as I did earlier in this section.

Quality Paperback Book Club, One Spirit Book Club, Fireside Theater Book Club, Stage and Screen Book Club, and Writer's Digest Book Club. He has been interviewed by or quoted in numerous publications, among them *Glamour, Redbook, Diablo Magazine,* the *San Francisco Chronicle,* and the *San Jose Mercury News,* and his books have been reviewed in *Publishers Weekly, Booklist, Library Journal, Variety, New Age Magazine, Intuition Magazine,* and *Common Boundary,* among many others.

For the past 15 years Maisel has counseled creative and performing artists in his creativity coaching practice, led classes and workshops, and taught in the management program at St. Mary's College (Moraga, California). He frequently presents to writers' groups (like the California Writers Club) and at writers conferences (among them the Mendocino Coast Writers Conference, the William Saroyan Writers Conference, and the Jack London Writers Conference).

Maisel actively markets his books through a variety of means, including his Creativity Newsletter, his website, via teleclasses, as an expert with Writers' Village University (where *The Creativity Book* is the text for three thousand students annually), and in talks to groups interested in human potential (like the Leading Edge). Maisel possesses undergraduate degrees in philosophy and psychology, master's degrees in creative writing and counseling, and a doctorate in counseling psychology.

Maisel is a California-licensed marriage and family therapist, a nationally certified counselor, and a novelist whose work has been reviewed in publications that include the *San Francisco Chronicle, Bestsellers,* and elsewhere. He lives in San Francisco, California, with his wife, Ann Mathesius Maisel, who is Associate Head of San Francisco's Lick-Wilmerding High School.[17]

---

[17] Some editors prefer that you don't put in any personal information, while others not only like it but feel that it makes a positive difference. In my actual proposal, I had included the following sentence:

Marketing Points[18]

- Maisel has appeared on national and local TV and national and local radio. During one recent two-week span he appeared on 30 national radio programs.

- Maisel's creativity books have always gone into multiple printings. *Fearless Creating* and *A Life in the Arts,* for example, are each in their eighth printings.

- Maisel's creativity books are highly praised and well-reviewed. For example: "Maisel's psychological approach sets his work apart" (*Library Journal*). *New Age Journal* called Maisel's *A Life in the Arts* "a fine, insightful work."

- The title will attract the large number of people interested in van Gogh. New van Gogh books are very popular, even when they are only a repackaging of his letters or another collection of his best-known paintings. Just as with *The Mozart Effect* or *How to Think Like Leonardo da Vinci,* where the author attached the name of a famous person to the points he wanted to make, *The Van Gogh Blues* conjures with the Dutch painter's well-known name.

- *The Van Gogh Blues* is a book that creativity coaches will want to purchase and recommend to their clients. The author is a leading trainer of creativity coaches and his online creativity coaching trainings attract participants from North America, Europe, and Asia.

"They have two daughters, Natalya and Kira, and four cats, Charlie, Bailey, Max and Sam." It's up to you whether or not to put in personal information. If you do put it in, remember to keep it brief, as the primary job of this section is to present the author's credentials as writer, promoter, and spokesperson, not as family man, cat owner, and so on.

[18] I consciously dubbed this section "marketing points" and not "marketing and promotion" because I meant to do only a minimal job of describing my prospective marketing efforts. Especially if you don't already have a track record as a published author, you will probably want to do a fuller job on this section of the proposal than I did, following the guidelines presented in chapter 8.

- The primary markets for *The Van Gogh Blues* are the estimated two million working creative and performing artists in America (National Council for the Arts figures), creators in other fields like science, technology, and business, and the millions more who dream of creating and take a personal interest in creativity.

Annotated Table of Contents[19]

Introduction. The premises of *The Van Gogh Blues* are presented: that all creative people suffer from bouts of depression, that the reasons for this are neither biological nor psychological but existential in nature, and that the only way for creators to manage their inevitable meaning crises and consequent depression is by learning to perform 10 core tasks.[20]

1. *Two Meaning Casualties.* In chapter 1 we meet Barry, a best-selling author, and Betty, a weaver, each in the throes of multiple meaning crises and consequent depression. These two vignettes portray the existential nature of creators' depression and set the stage for an examination of the first of the ten core tasks that creators need to master: reflecting on meaning.

2. *Reflecting on Meaning.* Barry, an unbeliever, and Betty, a believer, have different views about the universe but exactly the same job of

---

[19] In the proposal that was submitted, the annotated table of contents followed the sample chapter, which was the book's introduction. The introduction was strong, was chapter-length, and presented the book's basic ideas, so it felt like the right choice for sample chapter. I had originally anticipated that there would be 12 chapters, but when I began writing the book I saw that it required 14 chapters. As I had pledged a book of 75,000 words in length, that meant that I would need to keep each chapter to approximately 4,500 words when I wrote them.

[20] The method of summarizing I chose to employ is an abbreviated version of method 4, providing a narrative paragraph summary of each chapter. I felt that the succinctness and clarity of these brief summaries were positives that outweighed the possibility that I was not communicating enough information to a reader.

"forcing life to mean" what they decide it ought to mean. In order to do this metameaning work, they must step back and accomplish a task that most people recoil from in horror: actually reflecting on the meaning of their life.

3. *Meaningful Life, Meaningful Days, Meaningful Work.* In order for creators to experience their life as meaningful, they must maintain meaning in three distinct ways: the overall plan of their life must feel meaningful, the way they actually spend their minutes, hours, and days must feel meaningful, and the creative work they engage in must feel meaningful. In chapter 3 we see how difficult it is for creators to maintain meaning in all three of these spheres simultaneously.

4. *Opting to Matter.* Creators must act "as if" they matter if they are to maintain meaning and avoid depression, and they must do this even if they don't fully believe that they or their efforts matter. Furthermore, they must opt to matter in two different senses: in an egoistic sense, as the final arbiter of personal meaning, and in an ethical sense, in terms of living a principled life.

5. *Reckoning with the Facts of Existence.* Upsetness with the facts of existence, an upsetness experienced as anger, anxiety, sadness, or in some other visceral way, produces meaning crises and consequent depression. Creators have the task of disputing this upsetness, accepting reality, and, at the same time, meeting the facts of existence with exceptional resourcefulness, self-awareness, and courage.

6. *Forgiving Yourself and Others.* Creators have great difficulty making present meaning if they are consumed by resentment about the past and upset with themselves for their very human, very common failings. Therefore creators need to forgive themselves and others so as to release stored-up pain and disappointment. The idea of forgiveness as it relates to creative individuals and an examination of the practice of forgiving are the central subjects of chapter 6.

7. *Creating Worthily.* Creators need to use their innate talents on projects that they deem meaningful and that allow them to express their own ideas. Working solely on other people's projects is a path that is unlikely to allow a creator to sustain personal meaning. Every creator must also produce a full complement of his or her own creative work. The centerpiece of a meaningful creative life, creating personally worthy work, is the subject of chapter 7.

8. *Disputing Happy Bondages.* Many creators deal with their meaning crises in ineffective or unhealthy ways—tendencies that they need to dispute. Becoming addicted to some substance or behavior because the addiction is a happy bondage that acts as a meaning substitute is a typical but ineffective response to life's meaning crises. The down side of a happy bondage to alcohol, cocaine, sex—even to one's own creative efforts—is the subject of chapter 8.

9. *Relating to Others.* Creators need to relate if they are to maintain meaning. It turns out that a life of isolation and alienation, even a highly creative one, breeds depression by virtue of the fact that human meaning and human intimacy are intertwined. A lack of intimate relationships is a severe meaning drain, and creators must acknowledge that relating is as important as creating.

10. *Crafting Some Successes.* Creators need to experience some success if they are to experience life as meaningful. It is not possible to maintain meaning if a person finds herself defeated at every turn. But creators must define success in ways that take into account the facts of existence. If success to a creator means writing a bestseller, and if the odds against her book becoming a bestseller are thousands to one, then she will find herself in the throes of a meaning crisis the whole time she is waiting for that success to happen. In chapter 10, I examine how creators can redefine and revision the idea of success.

11. *Taking Action.* Meaning crises breed inaction and inaction exacerbates meaning crises. This common—and terrible—cycle regularly causes creative people to feel blocked, paralyzed, and defeated. They may spend years not creating, depressed the whole time, and not recognize that engaging in the smallest action in support of their creative life might interrupt the cycle and begin the process of meaning restoration.

12. *Rekindling Hope.* Psychotherapists believe that the goals of therapy are insight or insight coupled with behavior change. But a more fundamental goal is renewed hope. Each time hope returns in a creator's life, so does meaning. Learning how to maintain hope in the face of meaning crises and how to rekindle hope when hope is lost are vital tasks in a creator's life and the subject of chapter 12.

13. *Creating Your Personal Program.* In chapter 13 readers are instructed how to put together their personal program for meaning maintenance based on the 10 tasks described in the previous chapters. Examples of model plans, which take into account differences between the various creative disciplines, are described and explained.

14. *Becoming a Meaning Master.* Creators' depression is essentially a meaning problem, and the central solution is that each creator become his or her own meaning master. Creators need to learn how to recognize the ebb and flow of meaning in their life, what attitudes and activities maintain and restore meaning, and how they can commit to operating as their own personal meaning consultant around the clock. A creator who has mastered the intricacies of personal meaning-making will have the best chance of handling, and even avoiding, creators' depression.

Appendix: A Glossary of Meaning. Without a shared vocabulary of meaning it is very hard to discuss how some meaning events (like meaning drains, meaning leaks and meaning losses) cause depression, while other meaning events (like meaning investments, meaning opportunities, and meaning supports) help ease depression. In the appendix, 60 core terms are introduced and defined in a first-of-its-kind glossary of meaning.

ABOUT THE AUTHOR

ERIC MAISEL is a creativity coach and creativity coach trainer whose many books include *The Van Gogh Blues* (a Books for a Better Life Award finalist), *Fearless Creating, Deep Writing, The Creativity Book, Affirmations for Artists,* and *A Life in the Arts.* He is the editor of the Quotable Muse journal series (*Writers and Artists on Love, Writers and Artists on Devotion,* and others), creator of the Everyday deck series (*Everyday Calm, Everyday Creative, Everyday Smart*), a columnist for *Art Calendar* magazine, and a lecturer in the Institute of Transpersonal Psychology's coaching certificate program.

Maisel presents workshops at a wide variety of venues (among them the Savannah College of Art & Design and the Paris Writers Workshop) and holds a doctorate in counseling psychology, master's degrees in counseling and creative writing, and undergraduate degrees in psychology and philosophy. A California-licensed marriage and family therapist and a nationally certified counselor, he maintains a creativity coaching practice in San Francisco. He can be contacted via his website, www.ericmaisel.com.